SARAH WENTWORTH
MISTRESS OF VAUCLUSE

Carol Liston

Historic Houses Trust
NEW SOUTH WALES

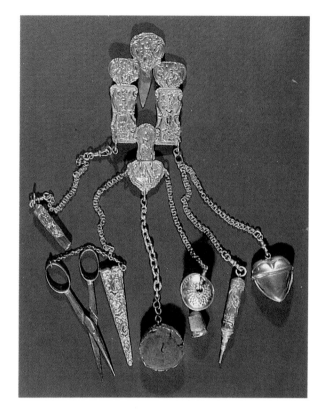

Sarah Wentworth's silver chatelaine, probably acquired during one of her visits to the Continent. *Vaucluse House Collection.*

Cover: Sarah Wentworth (1805-1880). *Private Collection.*

© Historic Houses Trust of New South Wales, Glebe, N.S.W. 1988

ISBN 0 949753 34 3
ISBN 0 949753 37 8 (Boxed Set)

Designed by Robin James
Typeset in 11/12½ Goudy by Tensor Pty Ltd
Printed by Nadley Press Pty Ltd

Contents

FOREWORD

THIS BOOK is one of a set of three the Trust has commissioned which examines the lives of the women who lived in three of the houses we are privileged to own. The other two books look at the lives of the four generations of women who lived at their home, Meroogal, in Nowra, and Elizabeth Macleay of Elizabeth Bay House and her six daughters. All three probe new areas of our history and we hope they will make a significant contribution to the history of women in this country.

The Historic Houses Trust acquired Vaucluse House in 1980 and immediately set about a major research project to find out as much as possible about the house and the principal family who had occupied it. This work has been largely undertaken by Joy Hughes with the advice and assistance of Ann Toy, curator of Vaucluse House since 1980. Together they have unearthed a wealth of material about Vaucluse House and the Wentworth family. Both confess to a growing affection and admiration for Sarah Wentworth as gradually their research revealed a woman of independence, substance and great courage.

Christine Eslick has carefully transcribed the Wentworth daughters' letters in the Mitchell Library. That Library's collection of letters and other Wentworth material was the principal primary source for this book. Descendants of Sarah and William Wentworth have been generous in allowing access to documents in their possession and we are grateful for their continuing generosity to Vaucluse House and the Historic Houses Trust.

Carol Liston has used this vast amount of material, and added to it information from her own research, to weave the extraordinary tale of the life of an extraordinary woman. She has done this with a skill that makes for compelling reading.

Many others have assisted and we thank them all: Mrs. Joan Weekes, Mr. Neville Wentworth, Mr. Dennis McCulloch, Mr. Bruce Todhunter, Mr. Don Fifer, Dr. James Broadbent, Miss Annette Macarthur-Onslow, Mr. Quentin Macarthur Stanham, National Parks and Wildlife Service, staff of the Mitchell Library.

We are also grateful to the following individuals and institutions for allowing pictures in their collections to be reproduced: The Hon. William Charles Wentworth, Mr. Neville Wentworth, Mrs. Eleanor Smith, Mrs. Christina Stephen, Mrs. Leila Ward, Mrs. Joanna Lillis, Major Patrick Durack, Mrs Elizabeth Curtis, Mr. Robert Hill, Mr. Don Fifer, Mr. Dennis McCulloch, Dr. John Dalhunty, National Library of Australia, Mitchell Library, Dixson Library and Dixson Galleries of the State Library of New South Wales.

Part of the funding for this series has been made available by the N.S.W. Government Bicentennial Secretariat and to it we are especially grateful.

PETER WATTS
Director
Historic Houses Trust of N.S.W.

INTRODUCTION

SARAH WENTWORTH performed no great deeds or good works, fought no battles for reform, left no legacy of treasures. Her biography was intended to celebrate her associations — she shared the bed of Our Greatest Patriot, bore his children and lived in a house that is now a National Treasure. Her story was the "private sphere", the hidden side of the career of William Charles Wentworth. As the project developed, it became clear that her biography offered new insights into the social life of colonial New South Wales, something more than mere background to political developments engineered by her husband. In the process most popular myths about the Wentworth family were overthrown.

Sarah's circumstances, in many ways, conformed to a series of stereotyped roles for colonial women. Yet in documenting the home life of Sarah and her children, there emerged new twists. Sarah was a currency lass but her convict father had left a legitimate family behind in Britain. Woven through Sarah's life is the connection with her father's other children. The "damned whore" perspective, usually limited to the convict period, is extended through Sarah Wentworth's experiences into the social traumas of the Victorian Age. The Wentworth girls, condemned as the off-spring of a damned whore, consciously or otherwise, conformed to the Victorian ideal of good and dutiful daughters, ministering angels to their father and brothers. Sarah was never permitted to play the role of politician's wife yet political events constantly impinged on her life. Understanding the domestic priorities of the Wentworth family clarify the reasons for Wentworth's retirement to England, leaving a leadership void for the conservatives on the eve of self-government. In England they established social contacts with retired colonists and former secretaries of state, all interested in Wentworth's comments on New South Wales.

I wish to thank the Historic Houses Trust of New South Wales for the opportunity to explore the rich variety of material on the Wentworth family. My especial and warmest thanks are to Joy Hughes who identified the most important sources, patiently transcribed Sarah's almost illegible letters and whose persistence uncovered many hidden resources and pictures of the family. My thanks, too, to Christine Eslick who transcribed the letters of the Wentworth daughters. Ann Toy, Curator of Vaucluse House, encouraged me to wander at will through Sarah's home and absorb its beauty. The final work, with its errors or omissions, remains my own.

CAROL LISTON

"this is all of little importance now but
when they undertake to write history
they ought to write the truth"

Sarah Wentworth to Thomas Fisher, 9 August 1871

CHAPTER ONE

Currency Lass

IN JANUARY 1810 the *Dromedary* brought a new governor to New South Wales. For the past two years the penal settlement had been confused by rebellion following the overthrow of its governor, William Bligh, by the officers of the New South Wales Corps. Lachlan Macquarie had been sent to re-establish law and order and aboard the *Dromedary* was a detachment of the 73rd Regiment to replace the rebellious New South Wales Corps.

For one private in the 73rd, the journey to the colony was also a personal quest. A Shropshire lad, John Cox had joined the regiment bound for New South Wales to search for his father. The family had heard nothing since he had been transported 20 years earlier, leaving behind his wife, three sons and an infant daughter. The three brothers were taught the family trade, blacksmithing, by their uncle but later joined the army. New South Wales in 1810 contained barely 10,000 individuals and John easily traced Francis Cox, the blacksmith. But his pleasure was tempered by the discovery that his father had a colonial family.

Francis Cox (or Cock) had arrived in Sydney in October 1791, a prisoner on the *Britannia*. Born about 1745, he had lived in the village of Broseley in eastern Shropshire. His trade, blacksmithing or ironworking, was a common one in the district. Many of the men from his village were employed at the nearby Coalbrookdale iron foundry where, in 1709, Abraham Darby had pioneered the use of coke to smelt iron, a technological breakthrough which heralded the start of Britain's Industrial Revolution. Coalbrookdale flourished throughout the eighteenth century; its innovations in ironworking and engineering reached new heights in 1779 with the casting of the first Iron Bridge, built across the Severn River near Broseley. Traditional blacksmithing skills were used in a variety of ironworking processes that were established near the Coalbrookdale foundry. These industries provided employment for Francis Cox and his brother, William.

John, eldest son of Francis Cox and his wife, Margaret, was baptised at St Leonard's church, Broseley in December 1783 and two boys, Samuel and Thomas, and a daughter, Ann, followed closely in the next seven years. Then disaster split the family. Perhaps, as his family suggested, a fondness

Francis Cox (c.1745-1831), father of Sarah Wentworth. *Copy held in Mitchell Library.*

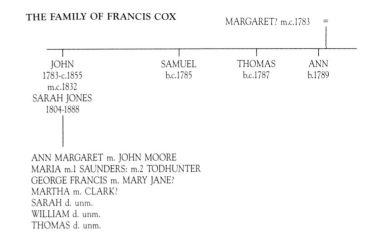

THE FAMILY OF FRANCIS COX

	MARGARET? m.c.1783 =

JOHN	SAMUEL	THOMAS	ANN
1783-c.1855	b.c.1785	b.c.1787	b.1789
m.c.1832			
SARAH JONES			
1804-1888			

ANN MARGARET m. JOHN MOORE
MARIA m.1 SAUNDERS: m.2 TODHUNTER
GEORGE FRANCIS m. MARY JANE?
MARTHA m. CLARK?
SARAH d. unm.
WILLIAM d. unm.
THOMAS d. unm.

for gambling led Cox to his downfall. Despite the prosperity of Broseley, Cox sought work as a labourer in Wolverhampton, a city in neighbouring Staffordshire. In late 1789, Cox returned to his home district. At 11 pm one November night, in the company of Thomas Abell, a labourer from Birmingham, Cox burgled two houses in the village of Madeley, across the Severn River from Broseley. They did not steal food or money but heavy, bulky items, taking more than 370 yards (338 metres) of woollen cloth, linen, muslin and printed calico and dozens of handkerchiefs, shawls and stockings from Jeremiah Baker. They stole similar goods from Thomas Godden.

Tried at the regional assizes in Shrewsbury on 13 March 1790, he was sentenced to seven years transportation to New South Wales. Carrying her baby daughter, Margaret Cox walked the 15 miles (24 kilometres) between Broseley and Shrewsbury to see her husband for the last time, then trudged back to Broseley and a bleak future. She and her children were left destitute, reliant on parish poor relief and the support of relatives. Her brother-in-law William and his sister, Sarah, helped raise the children.[1]

In New South Wales Francis Cox's skills as a blacksmith and his broader knowledge of ironworking were greatly in demand. When his sentence expired in 1797 he remained in Sydney where he formed an association with convict Fanny Morton.

Among the 131 female convicts who disembarked from the *Indispensible* in Sydney in April 1796 was Frances Moulton Cranmer. Possibly a native of Norwich, aged about 30, she had been arrested for stealing, tried at Middlesex Gaol Delivery in July 1795 and transported for life to New South Wales. Known as Fanny Moulton or Morton, she was probably assigned to

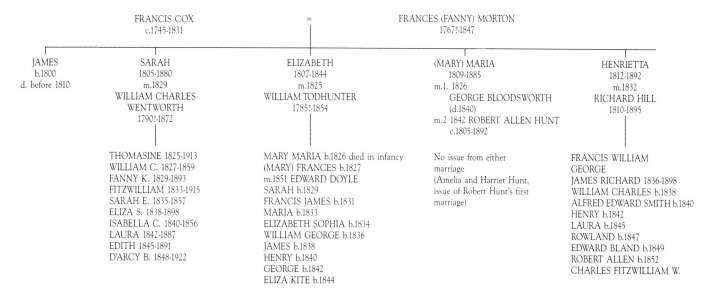

work as a domestic servant in Sydney where her duties, such as purchasing food and washing clothes, would have given her considerable freedom to roam the settlement.

Two years after her arrival Fanny was again in trouble. She was brought before the Sydney magistrates, charged with stealing a £5 promissory note from her companion, Charles Peat, and spending it at Campbell's store. Found guilty in July 1798, she was sentenced to death but her sentence was commuted to transportation to Norfolk Island. Fanny was, however, far advanced in pregnancy. The court ordered her into the custody of a constable and suspended her sentence until she recovered from the birth of her child. Six months later Fanny was again before the magistrates, this time accused by Mary Lewis of abusive language and obstructing her access to the public well. These charges were dismissed with a caution to keep the peace. In July 1799 Fanny was, for once, on the right side of the law when she successfully prosecuted a shoemaker for stealing leather she had given him to make her a pair of shoes. Her sentence of transportation to Norfolk Island apparently lapsed as no attempt was made to enforce it.[2]

The child born to Fanny in 1798 did not live. Nor did her next child, James, who was born on 21 September 1800 and died in childhood. His father was Francis Cox, the blacksmith. A daughter, Sarah Morton or Cox, was born on 1 January 1805 and baptised in September at St Philip's Church of England in Sydney. Three sisters followed — Elizabeth (b. 2 April

9

1807), Mary Maria (b. 6 November 1809) and Henrietta (b. 2 April 1812). As Francis Cox had a wife still living in England, he never married Fanny Morton, though she was commonly referred to as Mrs Cox.[3]

Francis, Fanny and the children lived on the waterfront in Sydney Cove where Cox had established his blacksmith's workshop, specialising as a ship and anchor smith. There was, as yet, no local industry to make iron and all metals were imported. Nor was there any manufacturing. Blacksmiths made all the metal implements and fittings required in the colony and repaired damaged items for metal objects were too valuable to discard. In the first two decades of settlement blacksmithing was controlled by the government to ensure that official requirements had priority. Cox was one of the first independent blacksmiths. By 1803 he had established a reputation as a skilled tradesman. Cox was in steady employment for the next three decades, servicing a growing maritime industry and winning tenders for ironmongery work on government buildings such as the gaol and the hospital. He employed journeymen and other smiths to assist him. A hard-working man, Cox lacked the entrepreneurial skills of some of his contemporaries and did not diversify his business interests. He maintained his family in modest comfort but was never a wealthy man. Nor did he take much interest in public affairs, apart from signing an address of welcome to Governor Bligh in September 1806 and distributing muskets to apprehend the pirates who seized the *Harrington* in 1808.[4]

His smithy was, in the first years of settlement, centrally placed at the government wharf just below Government House and not far from the government lumber yard with its large foundry. Later known as Cox's Wharf, Cox at first rented the land, then in 1806 he purchased it from Joseph Morley for £80. His land was bounded on the east by Macquarie Place and on the west by Sydney Cove and the Tank Stream. Cox and his family lived in a cottage adjoining the smithy. The premises were extended in the 1810s when the street frontage was properly formed and named Macquarie Place. By this time, Campbell's wharf on the western side of Sydney Cove had attracted most of the commercial traffic and Macquarie Place was a quieter route to the harbour. The Cox home was the last house before the waterfront. Their neighbours, some distance to the south, were Thomas and Mary Reiby, who in 1803 had built a house and store. Further along was Brown the merchant, the Reverend William Cowper's parsonage, Reuben Uther's hat factory and on the corner of Bridge Street, Simeon Lord's stores. By the 1820s Macquarie Place was a very respectable area, close to Government House and the homes and offices of the leading civil and military officials. A military band played regularly in its small park.[5]

Cox's business practices were not without blemish. The value of the

Sydney Cove in 1803. Francis Cox's residence which stood on the waterfront at the end of Macquarie Place, was possibly the small cottage to the right of the Government Wharf. Watercolour by John Lancashire. *Dixson Galleries.*

imported metals meant frequent thefts from the government stores. In November 1803 Francis Cox was charged with receiving a block of stolen iron, the property of the Crown. This he strenuously denied, arguing that he was unlikely to risk his hard-earned reputation for such a trivial offence. The iron that had been found in his house had probably been put there accidentally by Frances Morton who lived with him. He had instructed Fanny to gather up each evening any pieces of iron and tools lying around so that they would not be stolen. On this occasion Cox was acquitted. Six years later he was not so fortunate. In September 1809 he was found guilty of selling 80 pounds (36 kilograms) of government lead that had been left in his charge and sentenced to 12 months at the Coal River, Newcastle. During his absence, the smithy was probably let and Fanny and her daughters lived on a farm near Parramatta. Her third daughter was born two months after Cox was sentenced. Fanny and the children were at the farm when Private John Cox arrived in 1810.[6]

The two families of Francis Cox, one currency, the other sterling, were not unusual in colonial New South Wales. Many convicts lost contact with their families in Britain and established new relationships in the colony. John Cox found it difficult to accept that his father had abandoned his legal family in England and was living with another woman by whom he had a

11

young family. Nonetheless, when his father returned from Newcastle, John spent his leisure hours assisting him to re-establish the blacksmithing business and improve the house. John insisted that his mother, brothers and sister should share Francis Cox's modest success. By the time Private John Cox left the colony in March 1814, bound for Ceylon with his regiment, his father had agreed to make a regular allowance to his English family.[7]

Sarah Cox was five years old when she first met her half-brother. Though they were together only for four years, their fondness for each other endured throughout their lives. Most of the girls of Sarah's generation did not go to school. Despite the increase in population, the number of children attending school in 1819 was no larger than that in 1810. Sarah learnt to read and write but she never acquired an elegant hand, her sentences were rarely punctuated and her spelling erratic. Her family was not wealthy enough to employ a governess or to send the girls to one of the private academies that had by then been established. Sarah and her sisters probably received their formal education at one of the public charity schools established by Macquarie. The curriculum was limited to basic arithmetic, reading and writing, using the Bible and missionary literature as textbooks.[8]

The relative prosperity of colonial New South Wales and cheap convict labour meant that many currency lasses did not need to go out to work. Most remained at home, assisting in the house, the family business or farm until they married, usually by their twentieth birthday.[9] The daughters of blacksmith Francis Cox were not so fortunate. After a rudimentary education, Sarah Cox was apprenticed to a milliner when she was about 16. She moved from home and lived with her employer, Mrs Elizabeth Foster, a free emigrant who had opened a hat shop in Sydney about 1818.[10]

Francis Cox and his family were urban dwellers, living and working on the Sydney waterfront. He was never granted farming land, though he may have owned a small farm at Parramatta for a short time. Cox had no formal title to his Macquarie Place smithy and cottage until he was granted a lease in 1825, but two years earlier he had obtained a lease on a block of land on the east side of Phillip Street near the corner of Bent Street. Two small stone cottages were built on it. Francis Cox was then in his mid-seventies but, despite his "advanced and decrepit state of life", he still operated the smithy to support his aged wife and four daughters. He was not beyond claiming sympathy, implying that his English sons had died in the service of their country and left him without assistance in his old age. It was a ficticious appeal for compassionate treatment (his sons were alive in England) but he hoped that, if the government decided to resume his land, his appeal would ensure compensation and the grant of another waterfront block for his smithy and residence.[11]

CHAPTER TWO

Mistress

IN MAY 1825 Sarah Cox, aged 20, took an action in the Supreme Court of New South Wales against Captain John Payne for breach of promise of marriage. From 1818 to December 1823 Payne had commanded ships trading between Sydney and Port Dalrymple in Van Diemen's Land. Ship and anchor work was one of the specialities of Francis Cox and the sea captain probably met the blacksmith's daughter during business dealings with her father. The relationship between Sarah and Payne became serious in 1822 when Payne informed her parents and employer of his intentions to change her name to Sarah Payne. Her parents told him that Sarah had no fortune, to which he replied that he did not seek one. Payne continued plying the seas until the end of 1823 when he settled in Sydney. Life ashore extended his acquaintances and by March 1824 he had transferred his attentions to one of the daughters of wealthy emancipist merchant Edward Redmond. Payne, however, had no luck with Miss Redmond and returned to Sarah. Their quarrel was patched up and their marriage anticipated. Then Payne met Mrs Laverton, wealthy widow of William Laverton, a partner in the Lachlan and Waterloo flour mills.

The poor currency lass was once again rejected. Sarah accepted that Payne's affections had changed but when scandalous stories about her started circulating in Sydney, she accused Payne of injuring her reputation. Protesting that she was a respectable girl who kept good company and was never out late at night, Sarah took Payne to court. Her mother gave evidence of Payne's formal offer for Sarah's hand. Chief Justice Forbes instructed the jury with the leading comment that a promise of marriage had been deliberately given to her parents. The jury found in Sarah's favour, awarding her £100 damages and costs.[1]

This was the first time a case of breach of promise to marry had come before a jury in the colony, a fact not insignificant for the lawyers who took the case. Both were men intent on creating legal and political history. Dr Robert Wardell was Payne's lawyer; William Charles Wentworth represented Sarah. One of the witnesses, William Todhunter, a convict clerk engaged to Sarah's sister, denied that Sarah had become pale and haggard over the past

Left: Dr D'Arcy Wentworth (1762?-1827). *Private Collection.*

Below: William Charles Wentworth (1790?-1872), lithograph by J. Allan *(left)* and D'Arcy Wentworth (1793-1861) *(right)* sons of Dr D'Arcy Wentworth and Catherine Crowley. A third son John (b.1795) drowned in 1820 while serving with the Royal Navy. *Vaucluse House Collection.*

ten months. Yet it would not have been surprising if she was so. By May 1825 when she gave evidence about her injured reputation, Sarah and her lawyer were lovers and she was three months pregnant with his child.

Ten months earlier, in July 1824, the *Alfred* had sailed into Sydney Harbour. Its passengers had included Wentworth, returning to his native land after an absence of eight years studying in England. His father, D'Arcy Wentworth, had retired in 1819 as principal colonial surgeon but continued as treasurer of the Police Fund and manager of the colony's internal revenue until 1825. Though an important public figure and a wealthy man, D'Arcy Wentworth's private life excluded him from a central position in colonial society. He never married. His eldest son, William Charles, was born at Norfolk Island in mid-1790, the child of a convict woman, Catherine Crowley, who had been transported on the ship that D'Arcy sailed out in as surgeon. Two more sons, D'Arcy and John, were also born on Norfolk Island. In 1796 D'Arcy Wentworth, Catherine Crowley and the three boys settled at Parramatta where Catherine died in 1800, and three years later the two older boys were sent to school in England. About 1811 D'Arcy Wentworth formed a liaison with Ann Lawes, by whom he had eight children. Such relationships, though frowned upon by the more respectable settlers, were not unusual.

More important for assessing D'Arcy Wentworth's standing in the colony were the circumstances that led to his arrival in Australia. D'Arcy Wentworth was born in Ireland into the junior and impoverished branch of a distinguished Yorkshire family. The head of the family, Lord Fitzwilliam of Wentworth Woodhouse, acknowledged the Irish branch and used his influence on their behalf. While D'Arcy was studying medicine in London, however, he turned to highway robbery, either for adventure or to supplement his income. Brought before the Old Bailey in 1787 and acquitted, he was again in court in December 1789 and again found not guilty. At the end of the proceedings the court was informed that he had taken an appointment as assistant surgeon at Botany Bay and would leave immediately. Although he was never a convict, this brush with the law gave D'Arcy an ambivalent standing in the colony and he was often identified as an emancipist.

His son did not learn of this shadowy past until 1819. The revelations, made publicly in the House of Commons, caused some embarrassment and disillusionment. William abandoned his plan to marry into the Macarthur family as he recognised that his father's background made him socially unacceptable to them. He had just published an account of New South Wales in which he urged the extension of British constitutional practices and eventual self-government. Now he forged closer links with emancipist activists Dr William Redfern and Edward Eagar who were in London to

THE FAMILY OF D'ARCY WENTWORTH

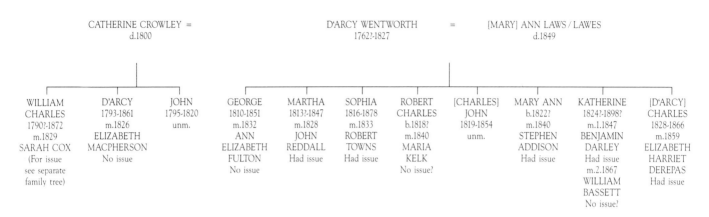

CATHERINE CROWLEY = d.1800			D'ARCY WENTWORTH 1762?-1827			=	[MARY] ANN LAWS / LAWES d.1849		

| WILLIAM CHARLES 1790?-1872 m.1829 SARAH COX (For issue see separate family tree) | D'ARCY 1793-1861 m.1826 ELIZABETH MACPHERSON No issue | JOHN 1795-1820 unm. | GEORGE 1810-1851 m.1832 ANN ELIZABETH FULTON No issue | MARTHA 1813?-1847 m.1828 JOHN REDDALL Had issue | SOPHIA 1816-1878 m.1833 ROBERT TOWNS Had issue | ROBERT CHARLES b.1818? m.1840 MARIA KELK No issue? | [CHARLES] JOHN 1819-1854 unm. | MARY ANN b.1822? m.1840 STEPHEN ADDISON Had issue | KATHERINE 1824?-1898? m.1.1847 BENJAMIN DARLEY Had issue m.2.1867 WILLIAM BASSETT No issue? | [D'ARCY] CHARLES 1828-1866 m.1859 ELIZABETH HARRIET DEREPAS Had issue |

promote the civil rights of ex-convicts. A third edition of his book, incorporating portions of the emancipist programme, was published in 1824 and he returned to New South Wales with Redfern as the native son triumphant.[2]

In September 1824 William Charles Wentworth was admitted to practise in the New South Wales Supreme Court. A gifted and able barrister, he quickly established a lucrative practice, earning over £1,500 in the latter half of 1825. Politically he indicated to settlers and officials alike his intentions to support the emancipist party's demands for traditional British liberties. In October 1824, with Dr Robert Wardell, a legal colleague and fellow passenger on the *Alfred,* he established the *Australian,* the first independent colonial newspaper. Wentworth relinquished editorial involvement within a year but for many years retained political credit as the champion of freedom of the press. By the end of 1824 he had also been elected a director of the Bank of New South Wales.[3]

Though his public life was an instant success, his private life reinforced the opinions of many free settlers about the immorality of the convict classes. Radical talk and heavy drinking encouraged people to think the worst. Helenus Scott met him at a dinner party in August 1824 and commented that he was a "downright radical…a very ungentlemanlike fellow" who would become a troublesome one.[4] Wentworth had taken rooms in Macquarie Place, close to Government House and the offices of senior officials, buildings which were guarded by military sentries. In February 1825 he was arrested by the sentries for wandering drunk in the city streets. This was not an isolated incident.[5]

Wentworth's first meeting with Sarah Cox was probably accidental. His office and lodgings were in Macquarie Place, near her parents' home, and they could easily have met in the street. Perhaps Mary Reiby, who had visited Wentworth in London in 1820, introduced the daughter of her neighbour to the colonial barrister.[6] Wentworth may even have deliberately engineered his association with Sarah Cox so that he could acquire information from her to use against John Payne. By early 1825 Wentworth was already acting as counsel for Bacon and Clayton to recover money from Payne, a former partner of Mathew Bacon. Payne, through his association with Mrs Laverton, had become a wealthy man, reputedly worth more than £5,000 and the owner of a mill and house at Kurrajong, a farm in Tasmania, a house in George Street and manager of a brewery. The breach of promise case allowed Wentworth to humiliate Payne.[7]

Though William Wentworth and Sarah Cox were both currency born with convict associations, they came from different worlds. Wentworth never mentioned his mother and probably barely remembered her, but his father was a rich man with aristocratic connections that enabled him to educate his sons in England as young gentlemen. Francis Cox had made a modest success of his life in New South Wales but his family moved among the lower ranks of respectable tradespeople, his daughters finding acceptable husbands among convict clerks and colonial born publicans. Elizabeth Cox, 18, married William Todhunter, aged 40, at St Philip's on 24 September 1825. Formerly a bank clerk in London where he knew Cox's family, Todhunter had arrived on the *Morley* in 1817 with a 14 year sentence. Maria Cox, 17, married George Bloodsworth, a colonial born publican, on 14 January 1826.[8]

After the breach of promise case, Wentworth sought a more private home than his rooms in Macquarie Place. In August 1825 he moved out to the Petersham estate on the road to Parramatta. Initially he rented the estate from Captain John Piper, but in September 1826 he paid £1,500 for the 295 acre (120 hectare) farm with its house, "a capital messuage or tenement", orchard and grazing paddocks. Sarah Cox moved to Petersham in mid-1825. Their child, Thomasine, was born there on 18 December 1825 in the midst of Wentworth's first major political triumph, a farewell dinner for the departing governor, Sir Thomas Brisbane. The baby was probably named after the governor. She was baptised at St James's Church on 15 January 1826, the daughter of Sarah Cox and W.C. Wentworth of Petersham.[9] At Petersham, Sarah and her baby lived in some comfort with several servants to attend them. Wentworth commuted between Petersham and his Sydney office, though he probably remained in town on many evenings because of the dangers of travelling at night. He was attacked on his way back to Petersham about 11 pm one spring evening in 1826 and some months later one of his servants was seized by intruders and searched. Such experiences must have been unsettling for town-bred Sarah.[10]

In a poem written in 1823 Wentworth had dreamed of:

the spacious harbour, with its hundred coves
and fairy islets — seats of savage loves[11]

Four years later, in June 1827, he acquired his own harbour cove. The 105 acres (42 hectares) at Vaucluse included "a genteel dwelling house" of eight rooms, stables, detached kitchen and dairy, gardens and orchards. The cottage had been built by Sir Henry Browne Hayes about 1803. Hayes (1762-1832) had arrived in New South Wales the previous year, transported from Ireland for kidnapping an heiress. A wealthy man, Hayes travelled out in relative comfort and despite frequent clashes with the colonial authorities lived with considerable freedom. In August 1803 he paid £100 for two farms, "a wild and uncultivated tract" on the edge of the harbour, which he named "Vaucluse" after the home of the mediaeval poet Petrarch. Here he created a "rustic little paradise", even surrounding the cottage with imported Irish turf which he hoped would retain its legendary attributes and repel snakes. The efficacy of this remedy was, however, exhausted by the 1860s when snakes were abundant at Vaucluse.[12]

Hayes lived intermittently at Vaucluse but the estate was leased from 1804 to his friend and confidant, Samuel Breakwell. Hayes and Breakwell both left the colony in December 1812 and Vaucluse was leased to Colonel Maurice O'Connell. After O'Connell was posted to Ceylon in 1814 the house was probably empty for a decade. Then in February 1822 it was acquired by Captain John Piper for £425 but he held it for only five years before it, along with his other possessions, had to be auctioned to meet his creditors' demands. W.C. Wentworth paid £1,500 for Vaucluse. In a subsequent transaction Wentworth exchanged land at Bathurst for Piper's title to a further 370 acres (148 hectares) adjoining Vaucluse and in January 1829 acquired Francis McGlynn's 40 acre (16 hectare) grant, thereby enlarging the Vaucluse estate to 515 acres (206 hectares) by 1829.[13] The cottage was, however, in poor condition so William and Sarah probably remained at Petersham for several months. Vaucluse had apparently been made habitable by November 1827 when tenants were sought for Petersham. A few months later Petersham was purchased by Robert Wardell. In May 1828 Wentworth commented that Vaucluse was "a very uncomfortable residence" but he was about to start his improvements.[14]

Shortly after William Wentworth purchased Vaucluse his father died. Aged 65 and one of the wealthiest men in the colony, D'Arcy Wentworth succumbed to an influenza epidemic. He provided for all his children, giving

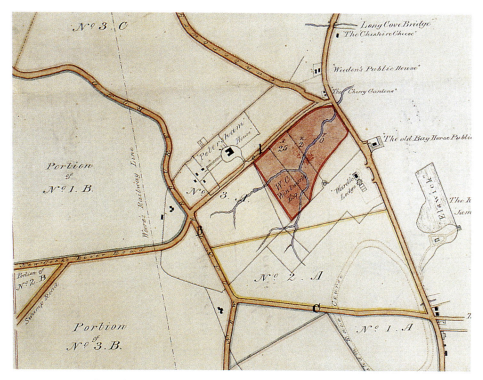

Petersham Estate in 1848, little changed since the late 1820s
when Sarah Cox lived there with William Charles Wentworth.
Wentworth Legal Papers. Mitchell Library.

them a life interest in various estates which would revert to his eldest son, William, if they died without heirs. William inherited land at Bringelly, one-seventh of his father's livestock and land in George Street valued at £5,000, which he immediately subdivided. It was a substantial inheritance. Overnight the rebel had become Mr Wentworth, landowner and barrister. He moved his law offices to George Street.[15]

In the months following his father's death, Wentworth's behaviour was reckless and offensive, not only to the government but to his friends. For many, he merely proved his reputation as "an infamous Blackguard, and in every respect worthy of his birth, his being the Son of an Irish Highwayman by a Convict Whore."[16] In the courts and in the papers, at public and private functions, he abused Governor Darling, accusing the governor of tyranny and threatening to impeach him over the death of a soldier. A violent tirade at the Turf Club dinner in November led Darling to threaten instant dismissal for any government officer found associating with Wentworth and Wardell. At 9.30pm on Sunday 16 December 1827, Wentworth was challenged by a military sentry who found him, somewhat intoxicated, wandering the streets of Sydney. His slurred reply when challenged to identify himself was that he was not Wentworth the attorney but Wentworth the barrister. And the governor was not the only person he had displeased. His role in the reconstruction of the Bank of New South Wales in late 1827 offended many wealthy emancipists and they rejected him at their annual anniversary dinner in January 1828. His relationship with Sarah Cox was also strained during these months. In the midst of his rampage, on 26 December 1827, Sarah gave birth to her second child. He was named William Charles but when baptised at St Philip's in January 1828, Sarah did not name the father and the child was registered as Cox.[17]

Vaucluse was an isolated spot, though plans were being made for a new road to the South Head, and its isolation was exploited in 1829 when Wentworth harboured an escaped convict there. Jane New, a convict, was arrested in December 1827 for theft. Released on bail, she met John Stephen when she came before the court on a shoplifting charge in August 1828. Stephen, a son of Judge Stephen and a friend and colleague of Wentworth, became infatuated with her. Jane lived with Stephen until her trial in January 1829 when she was sentenced to death. An appeal in March 1829, at which she was defended by Wentworth, commuted her sentence to confinement at her original place of transportation, Van Diemen's Land. Stephen arranged her escape from the Female Factory on 5 April 1829 and provided her with forged documents and shelter near Campbelltown. In mid-June the police learnt of her whereabouts but she fled before they arrived, finding refuge at Vaucluse. Stephen hoped to put her aboard a ship disguised as a boy but the authorities tightened their watch on departing vessels. Jane New remained hidden at Vaucluse for three weeks until, on 5 July 1829, she was smuggled aboard the *Emma Kemp*, bound for New Zealand, where she transferred to a whaler returning to England. John Stephen followed in another ship.[18]

Sarah Cox, in the early stages of her third pregnancy, was probably at Vaucluse during the three weeks that Jane New was hiding there. John Stephen had been employed as a clerk by Wentworth and he and his brother Francis were his regular drinking companions. Whatever the claims of friendship, Wentworth was taking a great risk in turning a blind eye to the runaway felon, if not actually contriving her escape. During these weeks it was reported that Wentworth was seriously ill at Vaucluse. Perhaps he *was* sick and unaware of the presence of Jane New; more likely, the illness was an excuse to keep visitors at a distance and avoid detection.[19]

Vaucluse prior to its acquisition in 1827 by W.C. Wentworth. Engraving from an
original drawing by James Wallis in his *Historical Account of the Colony of
New South Wales*, London, 1821. *Vaucluse House Collection.*

Whether Wentworth regarded the risks that Stephen took for Jane New
as a romantic adventure or a foolhardy infatuation is not clear, but it seems
that Stephen's dilemma forced him to look at his own private life and his
relationship with Sarah Cox. In September 1829 a poem by "W.C." was
published in the *Australian:*

To Sarah
For I must love thee, love thee on,
'Till life's remotest latest minute;
And when the light of life is gone, —
Thou'lt find its *lamp* — had *thee* within it.[20]

A month later Sarah Cox and William Charles Wentworth were married
at St Philip's Sydney. The witnesses were Robert Campbell junior, William's
friend and political supporter, and Elizabeth Todhunter, Sarah's sister. He
gave his age as 33 (though he was closer to 39), she gave hers as 23 (she was
24). The date, 26 October, was William's birthday (or rather the day on
which the family chose to celebrate his birthday as he probably never knew
the exact date or year). A month after their wedding, on 20 November 1829
their third child, Fanny Catherine, was born. She was named after her

21

convict grandmothers, Fanny Morton Cox and Catherine Crowley.[21]

There was no expectation that Wentworth should marry Sarah, though it was expected that if he left her he should make provision to support her and the children. His father, like many officials of his generation, had never married, perhaps because of a reluctance to make permanent connection with persons of lesser status. By the late 1820s, however, there were trends within both families for more regular relationships. William's brother D'Arcy was married in England in 1826; his half-sister had married the son of a colonial clergyman in 1828. Two of Sarah's sisters had also married. Wentworth's decision to marry Sarah Cox meant that he had finally rejected the advantages of an arranged marriage. In 1817, when he had sought to link himself with the Macarthur family through marriage, he had believed that:

> a union…between two families…having both in view objects of similar description, the formation of permanent respectable Establishments in the colony…[was] so essential…to the accomplishment of those projects for the future respectability and grandeur of our family.

By 1829 Wentworth was confident that his future lay in his own hands; he needed no dynastic alliance.[22]

Whatever the motivation to legalise their relationship, Wentworth was almost immediately unfaithful to Sarah. In January-February 1830 he had a brief liaison with Jemima Eagar. Her husband, Edward Eagar, was an emancipist lawyer who had gone to England in 1821 to further the emancipist cause. While there he had met Wentworth and collaborated on the third edition of his book. Eagar abandoned his family in the colony and never returned to New South Wales. A group of friends, including Wentworth, raised a trust fund to assist Jemima Eagar and the children. From 1828 Jemima and her children lived in a cottage owned by Wentworth. On 4 November 1830 Jemima Eagar gave birth to a son. The identity of the father was probably generally known, though the boy was not baptised for a decade. The father was then recorded as William Charles Wentworth.[23]

This is the clearest instance of infidelity; there may have been others. Contemporary references, usually from Wentworth's opponents, continued throughout the 1830s to proclaim him as a "champion of the convict classes to which he belongs…a man of immoral life and lowest origins".[24] His heavy drinking, short temper and coarse language provided plenty of evidence to reinforce such views.[25] Yet while Wentworth showed no restraint in his own behaviour, his expectations of Sarah's conduct as his wife were clear. In a speech in January 1833 Wentworth, in alluding to the right to trial by jury, commented that "the fountain of justice, like a man's wife, should not only be unpolluted but unsuspected."[26]

CHAPTER 3

Wife and Mother

SARAH WAS THE WIFE of one of the most prominent men in colonial Australia, yet she was unknown to many of her contemporaries. Wentworth's behaviour did not encourage close personal ties and her background as his mistress restricted their social life to their family circle. A calm, determined and practical woman, devoted to "my kind husband", she was the perfect foil to his more passionate temperament.[1]

Sarah was not well after Fanny's birth and suffered three miscarriages in the next two years. Sarah and William's second son, Fitzwilliam, was born at Vaucluse on 31 July 1833 and baptised at St Philip's the following month. Five daughters followed — Sarah Eleanor (b. 2 August 1835), Eliza Sophia (b. 24 October/November 1838), Isabella Christiana, (b. 20 September 1840), Laura (b. 12 November 1842) and Edith (b. 1 January 1845). Their tenth child and third son, D'Arcy Bland Wentworth, was born on 10 January 1848. Sarah, now in her mid-forties, was pregnant again in 1850 but the child, a daughter, was stillborn.[2]

The children were born at Vaucluse, probably with Sarah's mother, sisters and a midwife assisting and Wentworth's friend and political colleague, Dr William Bland, standing by in case of emergency. A large family, with a child born every two or three years, was usual, the pattern determined by the natural contraceptive effect of breast-feeding each baby for 12 to 15 months. Sarah was more fortunate than many of her contemporaries in that all her children survived infancy, childhood illnesses and accidents. With a family spread over 25 years, the older children were of similar ages to their father's half-brothers and sisters (D'Arcy Wentworth's last child was born posthumously in 1828) and the youngest children were the same age as Sarah's older grandchildren, the first of whom was born in 1844. Family Christian names were common so pet names were used to avoid confusion between children and adults with the same names. Sarah's daughter Sarah Eleanor was usually known as Joody and Eliza was called Didy to distinguish her from her aunt, Mrs Eliza Wentworth, the wife of Major D'Arcy Wentworth.

Sarah and William had a large extended family. Wentworth's half-brothers, half-sisters, cousins and their families and Sarah's sisters, husbands

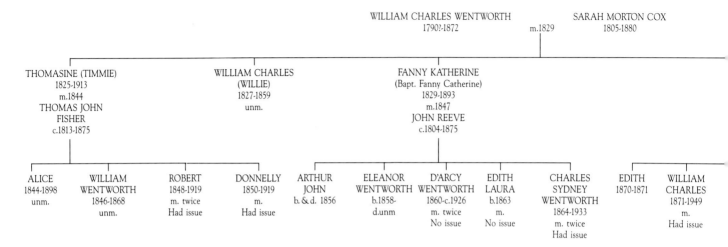

WILLIAM CHARLES WENTWORTH
1790?-1872
m.1829
SARAH MORTON COX
1805-1880

THOMASINE (TIMMIE)
1825-1913
m.1844
THOMAS JOHN
FISHER
c.1813-1875

WILLIAM CHARLES
(WILLIE)
1827-1859
unm.

FANNY KATHERINE
(Bapt. Fanny Catherine)
1829-1893
m.1847
JOHN REEVE
c.1804-1875

ALICE
1844-1898
unm.

WILLIAM
WENTWORTH
1846-1868
unm.

ROBERT
1848-1919
m. twice
Had issue

DONNELLY
1850-1919
m.
Had issue

ARTHUR
JOHN
b. & d. 1856

ELEANOR
WENTWORTH
b.1858-
d.unm

D'ARCY
WENTWORTH
1860-c.1926
m. twice
No issue

EDITH
LAURA
b.1863
m.
No issue

CHARLES
SYDNEY
WENTWORTH
1864-1933
m. twice
Had issue

EDITH
1870-1871

WILLIAM
CHARLES
1871-1949
m.
Had issue

and their children were frequent visitors at Vaucluse and provided a network of social companions and business associates. Sarah's parents probably lived at Vaucluse. When her father became ill in 1831 he was moved back to Sydney, close to doctors and his other daughters. He was nursed at Maria and George Bloodsworth's home in Sussex Street and Sarah came in from Vaucluse each day to sit with him. His right leg was amputated to prevent infection spreading but it was too late. Word was sent to Fanny Cox at Vaucluse and she and her four daughters gathered at his bedside. Francis Cox died on 17 June 1831, aged 86, "an old and much respected inhabitant". He was interred in the Sandhills cemetery but Wentworth promised Sarah that ground would be consecrated at Vaucluse so that her father could be buried there in a family vault.

In his will, Francis Cox left to his wife Fanny his personal effects and a life interest in all rents from his properties. The two cottages on the corner of Bent and Phillip Streets were bequeathed to his sons-in-law, William Todhunter and George Bloodsworth, and Sarah and Henrietta, both unmarried when the will was written, inherited the house and smithy in Macquarie Place. Furthermore, if his English son, John Cox, came to the colony within three years of his father's death, John was to inherit the blacksmithing tools and occupy the workshop for his lifetime. After the death of Francis Cox, Fanny divided her time among her daughters and grandchildren, living intermittently at Vaucluse. She died, aged 80, on 17 October 1847 in the Phillip Street house, home then of R.A. Hunt, Maria Bloodsworth's second husband.[3]

Sarah's attitudes to her children (and perhaps the secret of her success

THE FAMILY OF SARAH AND WILLIAM CHARLES WENTWORTH

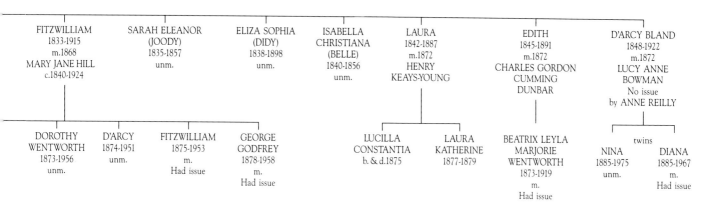

with her husband) were expressed most clearly in her advice about the upbringing of her grandchildren. Children were like servants: it was no use constantly arguing or trying to force them against their will.

> if he is made with a will of his own you must yeald and use all your efforts to guide him not by continually lecturing him for that with all of us will lose its effects....I am quite sure pushing too much is not the way to make others do all you wish.[4]

The children shared many characteristics, physically and temperamentally, of their father and he was the central figure in all their lives. Sarah was delighted on visiting York Minster in later years to see the strong family resemblance between her daughter Laura, Wentworth's cousin Martha Bucknell and the Wentworth effigies in the cathedral.

> I consider my children have a strong will of their own and not the best tempered but I am sure they would almost lay down their life for their Father and he no doubt would have great power if it was required to make them do whatever he wished and you know how indulgent he is[5]

Sarah raised at least one of her nieces. Mary Frances Todhunter, born in 1827, was the eldest surviving daughter of Sarah's sister Elizabeth Todhunter. Sarah brought up Mary until she was about 18 when her mother died in childbirth and Mary presumably returned home to care for the younger children. Mary married Edward Doyle in 1851 but it was not a happy marriage and Sarah, who retained a great affection for Mary throughout her life, helped support Mary and her children.[6]

William Charles Wentworth was effectively the guardian of eight younger half-brothers and sisters, the children of his father and Ann Lawes, who lived at Parramatta until her death in November 1849. With an age difference of 20 years between William and his eldest half-brother, George Wentworth of Greendale (b. 1810), William was almost a second father to the younger children — Martha (b. 1812), Sophia (b.1816), Robert (b.1818?), John (b.1819), Mary Ann (b. 1822?), Katherine (b. 1824?) and Charles (b.1828). George was paid by his brother until 1831 to manage the properties left by D'Arcy Wentworth. The following year he married Anne Fulton, daughter of the Reverend Henry Fulton. George had inherited a tenth share in his father's personal estate, valued at about £10,000, but he lost most of his property in the depression of the 1840s.[7]

Robert, aged 15 in 1833, and John Wentworth (13) returned to Sydney in December 1833 after some years at school in England. W.C. Wentworth kept a strict watch on their behaviour. He sent John back to England in 1840 to his agent, Robert Brooks, with instructions that he be taught something of farming. Brooks outfitted him at Wentworth's expense and placed him with one of the best wool brokers in London for six months. Anxious to return to the colony, John was sent back on the *Duke of Roxburgh* in mid-1841, again at his brother's expense. Brooks commented that he had not noticed the "tendency to the habit" which Wentworth had feared the boy had acquired in the colony and added that he needed to have "active employment with some little responsibility placed on his own shoulders". John did not settle into colonial life and a year later Wentworth sent him to Cambridge University, despite his doubts that John had any serious interest in academic life, for he considered him interested only in "profligacy and dissipation". John Wentworth's shortcomings were a constant warning to Wentworth's eldest son, Willie, eight years John's junior.[8]

Wentworth supervised the lives of his half-sisters with similar watchfulness, paying for their tuition and clothing until their marriages. Sarah had been drawn into their upbringing even before her marriage to Wentworth. In January 1828 she purchased clothing for Martha Wentworth, born in 1813. A few months later Martha married John Reddall, son of the Reverend Thomas Reddall.[9] In December 1833 Sophia (aged 17) and Mary Ann Wentworth (11) returned from school in England aboard the *Brothers*, captained by Robert Towns whom Sophia married a week after landing in Sydney. Mary Ann probably divided her time between her mother at Parramatta and her brothers and sisters. She was living at Vaucluse in December 1840 when William Charles Wentworth consented to her marriage to Captain Stephen Addison.[10]

Another member of the family circle was Martha Bucknell, nee Wentworth, a niece of D'Arcy Wentworth who had migrated to Australia from Ireland. Martha and her watchmaker husband, William, lived at Newtown. She frequently stayed with William, Sarah and the children at Vaucluse. Wentworth provided financial support for Bucknell, especially when Bucknell became insolvent in the 1840s.[11]

W. C. Wentworth was closest to his full brother, D'Arcy, who was born on Norfolk Island in 1793. Their other brother, John, went to sea and drowned in 1820. D'Arcy had enlisted in Macquarie's regiment, the 73rd, and was stationed in Britain when his father died in 1827. In Scotland on 27 April 1826 he had married Elizabeth Macpherson, daughter of the late Major Charles Macpherson, Barrack-Master General for Scotland. D'Arcy transferred to a regiment serving in Australia and was stationed in Sydney and Launceston. He inherited his father's Toongabbie estate and made his home there when he was in Sydney. D'Arcy was member for the Northumberland Boroughs, representing East and West Maitland and Newcastle in the New South Wales Legislative Council from June 1843 to August 1845. As Toongabbie was let during these years, he and his wife lived at Vaucluse with Sarah and William. Unable to have children of her own, Eliza Wentworth was very fond of her nephews and nieces and was Sarah's mentor.[12]

Most of Sarah's social life, and much of her husband's business life, involved family members. Wentworth's financial interests had increased greatly with his father's death. D'Arcy, a full-time soldier, had little interest in farming or business and their half-brothers had inherited considerable wealth of their own. They were not dependent on Wentworth and, in any case, were too young and lacked the skills needed to manage his affairs. In seeking management assistance Wentworth turned not to his own family, but to Sarah's. Patronage established in the 1820s was reinforced by the marriages of Sarah's sisters and, later, of her nephews and nieces.

Sarah's brother-in-law, William Todhunter, was a convict clerk in the commissary's office and acted as Wentworth's agent in business matters even before his marriage to Sarah. From the mid-1830s he was resident manager for Wentworth's Hunter Valley properties and his sons were later employed on Wentworth's north-western squatting stations.[13] Henrietta Cox, Sarah's youngest sister, married Richard Hill in January 1832. The son of an emancipist and a carpenter by trade, Hill had managed the Vaucluse estate and Wentworth's city properties before his marriage and continued to do so until the mid-1860s. With his brother George, who later became mayor of Sydney, he ran a slaughter house, butcher shop and public house in Sydney. This became an outlet through which Wentworth's cattle were sold. Sarah encouraged these business arrangements and was frequently at the butcher shop, though it was unlikely that she worked there, as her critics alleged.[14]

Maria's first husband, George Bloodsworth, died in 1840 and two years later she married widower Robert Allen Hunt, a senior officer at the General Post Office in Sydney from 1833 until his retirement. Hunt acted as agent for Wentworth from the late 1840s. Amelia and Harriet Hunt, his daughters by his previous marriage, were welcome guests at Vaucluse.

As early as 1831 Sarah and William had considered the question of educating their children in England. Expectation was strong that Wentworth's political ambitions would take him to England in the mid-1830s but his pastoral affairs were at a critical stage of expansion, requiring close supervision, and so the children went to school in the colony.[15] Wentworth was a strong supporter of secular education and in 1835 became a shareholder in the new Sydney College, a non-denominational school with a classical curriculum designed to prepare boys for higher education in England. The headmaster from 1835 to 1842, W. T. Cape (1806-1863), was one of the few intimate friends of the Wentworth family and his wife and children visited informally at Vaucluse. William Charles Wentworth, junior, known to the family as Willie, attended Sydney College, possibly as a day boy while the family lived at Vaucluse but certainly as a border in his senior years when the family was often at its Hunter Valley estate. Willie was taught Latin, Greek, French, mathematics, literature and history. At the end of 1842, when he was 15, he took his final examinations in classics and mathematics, winning the school medal for classics.[16]

Fitzwilliam, known as Fitz, was six years younger than Willie and attended the Normal Institution near Hyde Park. This school, established by the Reverend Henry Carmichael in 1834 to train schoolteachers, was non-denominational and stressed critical thinking and a liberal approach to religion. Classes included English, jurisprudence and political economy. Physical development was as important as mental skills and the boys were instructed in gymnastics and military drill. In 1842, as a nine-year-old, Fitz studied classics, French, Latin and history. His schoolmates included his relatives, the Hills and Bucknells. The Normal Institution closed in 1843 and Fitz transferred to Elfred House, a new academy that had been started by William Cape in Glenmore Road, Paddington in 1842. It was an expensive school, with fees of £12.10.0 per quarter.[17]

Sarah, with her limited education, did not possess the necessary accomplishments to teach her daughters herself. Her household probably included a governess, but in the late 1830s Thomasine and Fanny were sent to day schools in Sydney and then probably attended a boarding school in the early 1840s. Thomasine (Timmie to her family) left school in 1842, when she was 17, and married soon after. Education for girls was less academically rigorous than for boys, concentrating on lady-like skills such as music,

The Normal Institution, Sydney, a secular school favoured by the Wentworths
for the education of their son Fitzwilliam. Engraving by J. Carmichael in
J. Maclehose *Picture of Sydney... 1839*, Sydney, 1839.

dancing, painting, needlework and some foreign languages. Timmie and
Fanny acquired the accomplishments expected of young women of wealth —
they sketched with coloured crayon and water paints; they played the piano
and the guitar; when horses were available they rode. Their little sisters
played with dolls and enjoyed the gardens of Vaucluse and Windermere,
their Hunter River estate.

Clothing seven girls required constant sewing. Sarah's accounts recorded
the yards of fabric, laces and ribbons, the bonnets, gloves and shoes
purchased for her daughters. Clothes for the younger children were often
bought ready-made in Sydney but the older girls had their clothes made by
dressmakers in town or by Sarah herself with the assistance of a needlewoman. Sometimes the sewing work was sent to the convict women at the
Parramatta Factory. A tailor lived intermittently at Vaucluse to make the
suits of corduroy and colonial tweed preferred by Wentworth and to mend
and alter clothes for the boys.[18]

In these years Sarah was mistress of two family homes — Vaucluse and,
from 1836 to 1848, Windermere, near Maitland. Despite its almost rural
isolation, Sydney already encroached on Vaucluse. Though there were few
houses along the harbour foreshores, on a summer evening or weekend the

29

people of Sydney thronged to the heights above Vaucluse to breathe the fresh air, admire the wild flowers and birds and enjoy the view of the harbour, always busy with shipping. The new South Head road, built closer to the harbour in the early 1830s, was a flat sandy track flanked by large trees inhabited by noisy black cockatoos. Harbour views appeared "like a succession of pictures through a natural framework of gum trees and acacias", with here and there a residence with shady gardens overlooking the small bays.[19]

Vaucluse gained some notoriety when Governor Darling left New South Wales in 1831. Wentworth's quarrel with Darling was both political and personal and he had promised to avenge himself on the day Darling departed. On the afternoon of Wednesday 19 October 1831 Wentworth held a public fete at Vaucluse to celebrate the recall and imminent departure of Darling. The day before, a fatted ox decorated with ribbons was led through the streets of Sydney and the populace was invited to bring their knives and forks to a banquet at Vaucluse. A crowd, variously estimated between two and four thousand adults and children, flocked to Vaucluse to feast on the bullock, 12 sheep roasting on a spit in front of the house and 4,000 loaves of bread washed down with tubs of Cooper's gin and Wright's beer. Such "orgies of the lowest rabble of Botany Bay, congregated in the open air, shrouded by the curtain of night" were, in the eyes of the self-righteous, just the behaviour that they would have expected of Wentworth. Most of the crowd returned to Sydney at dusk but it was a fine moonlit evening and many lingered to enjoy a "gin-erous" night of "rustic sports". At 7pm bonfires, visible in Sydney, were lit on the hill behind Vaucluse while in town buildings were illuminated with slogans such as "Down with the tyrant". Wentworth's home was not opened to the crowd and Sarah and the children probably watched the entertainments from the house — and endured the mess left behind in the rain of the next few days.[20]

When Wentworth purchased Vaucluse in 1827, the house was an uncomfortable single storey rubble stone cottage of eight rooms. Renovations started in mid-1828 but the convict painter lent to Wentworth by his friend Dr H.G. Douglass was arrested within a fortnight as a runaway convict, leaving the drawing room decorations incomplete.[21] In March 1829 George Cookney was commissioned to erect a "splendid suite of outbuildings". Cookney, son of D'Arcy Wentworth senior's, English agent, was a boyhood companion of William Wentworth. He had migrated to New South Wales in 1825 and worked briefly as colonial architect before turning to private commissions. Imposing Gothic stone stables with seven stalls, coach house, harness room, men's quarters and a large loft were built east of Vaucluse House. Further to the east was a large stone barrack, quarters for convict servants.

The Vaucluse Estate in the 1840s with its house and adjacent
stables *(lower left)* and convict barracks *(mid-foreground)*.
Oil painting by G.E. Peacock. *Mitchell Library.*

Work started on a rebuilding programme to create a "new and elegant
chateau". Extensions around the core of the old cottage added a dining
room and bedrooms on the west and a winter sitting room and a small
drawing room on the east, its french windows opening onto a verandah. At
the back of the house was a new wing with an enormous kitchen, scullery,
larder and dairy, offices for the butler and housekeeper, domestic quarters
for the servants and a schoolroom on the first floor. By the early 1830s a

31

stone laundry, separate storeroom, guard room and boat house completed the range of outbuildings at Vaucluse.[22]

Further extensions in the Gothic style were added in the late 1830s. A three storey wing built parallel to the kitchens was linked to the house by a stair hall dominated by a castellated tower. A matching eastern tower with entrance portico was planned but not built when the depression and bank crises of the 1840s absorbed all available cash. Vaucluse emerged looking not unlike the plans proposed for the new Government House. Wentworth was friendly with Governor Bourke and may have seen the Government House plans when they arrived in 1834.

On the ground floor of the new wing, close to the kitchen, was a breakfast room. The children soon left their mark here — someone scratched "my dear Tomisine" on the marble fireplace. Wentworth's office and study was next to the gate leading to the outbuildings. Beneath these rooms were cellars, elaborately fitted out for wines and food storage. On the first floor was the principal bedroom and an adjoining sitting room. The children slept on the floor above — one room was shared by the older girls, there was an adjoining nursery bedroom and the older boys, when not away at school, shared a room formed by enclosing the eastern end of the upper hallway.

Vaucluse had no formal entrance. Visitors entered the grounds from the east and found themselves in a kitchen courtyard flagged with sandstone. The "woman's room", the province of Sarah and her housekeeper, looked out on the courtyard. From here tradesmen turned left to the kitchen wing, while family visitors turned right, entering a long narrow hall floored with black and white marble. From here they were shown into the drawing room where the ladies of the house received visitors, took morning and afternoon tea and gathered before dinner. Excluded from the formal round of carefully contrived, strictly timed social visits of colonial Sydney, the lifestyle of the women at Vaucluse was probably more informal than that of their contemporaries.

Sarah managed her family, the servants, both convict and free, and the grounds of Vaucluse. Hers was not a pioneer existence of manual toil. Her home and its grounds were well-established when she moved to Vaucluse in 1828 and her husband was able and willing to pay for any servants that she wanted. Among the convict women assigned to Vaucluse in 1832 were three laundresses, a needlewoman and two general servants though by 1841 Sarah employed only free women. The household staff in 1844-45 included Louisa, the highest paid servant who was probably the housekeeper; Harriet and Mary the needlewomen; a nurse to help with the children; housemaids; a laundress; and Mary Barker, the cook. Others were hired as needed, whether it was extra help in the laundry or the occasional tailor, carpenter or blacksmith for a few days' work. Outdoor staff included a coachman, George the groom and Clark the gardener.[23]

West of the house, beyond the kitchen gardens of vegetables and herbs, were vineyards and an orangery. Long-established orchards continued to flourish, supervised by Sarah who was fond of gardening. They kept a house cow and some poultry and grew a little lucerne for green feed. Sarah later recalled that her husband would not let her have goats.[24] A practical woman, Sarah dealt easily with the difficulties of household drains, flooded cellars and broken fences. She was a methodical housekeeper too, aware of the need for inventories to manage a large household on the move, whether between Vaucluse and Windermere or, in later years, between Brussels, Paris and London.[25]

Vaucluse was relatively close to Sydney, so it was usually more convenient to purchase food than to rely on home produce especially when the family spent half the year away at Windermere. Vegetables were home-grown but most other foodstuffs were purchased, the largest expense being the meat bill. Bread, potatoes, rice, flour, corn, yeast, ducks, lobsters, dried fruit, oil and even eggs were bought in town. Though the kitchen staff may have made their own tallow candles, Sarah paid £5.8.0 for one supply of best quality sperm candles for the house. Starch, mops, buckets and kitchen items were bought in Sydney shops for both Vaucluse and Windermere.[26]

When Wentworth returned to New South Wales in 1824 there had not been sufficient lawyers in the colony to justify a division between solicitors and barristers, and he established a lucrative practice in both areas. In September 1829 the Supreme Court decided that only barristers trained in Britain would be permitted to appear before the court. British approval of this change was not received until October 1834, a few weeks after Wentworth's friend and colleague Robert Wardell was murdered. Wentworth practised at the bar for another year but his income had been significantly reduced by the new policy which excluded him from working as a solicitor. From 1834 he devoted more time to managing his pastoral investments and did not practise as a barrister after October 1835.[27]

Land grants had ceased in 1831. Between 1832 and 1839 Wentworth purchased 39,094 acres (15,820 hectares) of Crown land for cash payments of £12,245. Most of this land, 24,811 acres (10,000 hectares), was in the County of Brisbane in the upper Hunter Valley, with smaller portions in the neighbouring counties of Durham and Northumberland and some large areas in the western counties of Bathurst and Roxburgh. He also invested in land at Port Phillip. A bushman and explorer from his youth — he had been one of the first party to cross the Blue Mountains in 1813 — he had a good eye for land and selected well.[28]

33

These widespread acquisitions meant that Wentworth was often up-country, leaving Sarah to manage the family and Vaucluse. Wentworth was a hard master and Sarah's greatest difficulties were managing the convict servants, who were often insolent to the family while Wentworth was away. Brought before Wentworth on his return and threatened with the magistrates, the convicts invariably absconded. When caught some months later, the magistrate usually gave the runaways 25 lashes and sent them back, unrepentant, to Vaucluse. Wentworth demanded 50 lashes as punishment for his runaway servants. From the mid-1830s, this problem faded as most of their assigned convicts worked in the country. Of 61 convicts assigned to Wentworth in 1837, only two were in Sydney. The 1841 census recorded 31 adults in the Wentworth household at Vaucluse. All but 12 were listed as free. There were no convict women but three ticket of leave and nine assigned male convicts.[29]

The decline in the number of convict servants in their home was probably a result of an incident in 1835. On the evening of 14 October 1835, six assigned servants broke into the storeroom at Vaucluse and stole flour, sugar and tobacco and a plate chest containing about £100 worth of spoons, forks, ladles and small pieces of silver. They fled to Vaucluse Bay where they joined three convicts from the lighthouse and seized the *Alice*, Wentworth's 20 tonne cutter. Among the possessions they left behind, Sarah found a packet of poison. Wentworth was convinced they had planned to murder him because some weeks earlier he had punished one of the runaways for drunkenness and insolence. The pirates headed north with the revenue boat in pursuit and were eventually caught near Port Stephens. Wentworth thus lost the services of a house servant, tailor, cooper, bricklayer and two labourers. All had been transported for life.[30]

From 1836 Wentworth and his family lived in the Hunter Valley for part of each year. Wentworth owned most of Gammon Gammon Plains, near Merriwa, in the County of Brisbane. He extended his holdings in July 1836 by purchasing Governor Brisbane's adjoining 10,000 acre (4,000 hectare) grant. Gammon Gammon Plains, ideal for grazing with its open grass lands, was on the outskirts of settlement, in the farthest of the 19 counties to which landholding was restricted. With so much of his capital invested in the upper Hunter Valley, Wentworth needed a base nearby to supervise it personally rather than rely on resident superintendents. In May 1836 he purchased from T.M.W. Winder (1789?-1853), for £25,000, Windermere and Luskintyre, adjoining estates near Maitland.[31]

Windermere was conveniently close to transport. Sarah and the children could travel comfortably by steam boat from Sydney to Newcastle, along the Hunter River to Morpeth, near Maitland, then continue by carriage to

Harpur's Hill, 1841. Pencil sketch by Conrad Martens thought to
have been commissioned by W.C. Wentworth. *Mitchell Library.*

Windermere. Heavier items were freighted by the overland route through
Wollombi. From Lochinvar and Windermere the road up the Hunter Valley
climbed over Harpur's Hill to Branxton and on to Muswellbrook where the
road branched to Merriwa. Wentworth reputedly spent £4,000 building a
thirty room shingle-roofed home, "a commodious family mansion...tastefully
designed, elegantly finished in the best style of workmanship". The house
was on the crest of the ridge and utilised the abrupt fall of the land toward
the river for basement servants' quarters and extensive cellars. With eleven
bedrooms, a double kitchen, dining and drawing rooms, Windermere was
probably more comfortable for his growing family than Vaucluse. A two
storey brick stable, coach house and outbuildings completed their facilities.[32]

For the next decade Sarah moved her family each year to Windermere for
late winter and spring, returning south to Vaucluse for summer. They were
usually at Windermere for October, the important month for the pastoralist
when the rams were put to the flock for a March lambing and when
shearing started. In the 1840s Wentworth acquired more stations along the
Hunter River, including Belltrees near Scone, and land at Lamb's Valley.
Belltrees became the central woolwash for Wentworth's flocks. Here in the
mid-1840s about 180,000 sheep were mustered and run through the river to

wash their fleeces before shearing.[33] When Wentworth entered parliament in 1843, Sarah and the children often remained at Windermere through the winter and spring while William stayed in Sydney for the sittings of the Legislative Council. Vaucluse was closed up and he lived in lodgings in town. Wentworth, a doctor's son, would not move his family to Windermere permanently and let Vaucluse because he became "uneasy and fidgety" whenever Sarah or the children were ill "and the idea of having no residence to bring them within reach of medical assistance would make him... quite miserable".[34] Sarah returned to Vaucluse for the births of her children.

Timmie, their eldest daughter, found life at Windermere very dull. There was no piano and they were out of reach of any news. The monotony of country life was broken only by horse riding, visits to nearby estates, drawing and an occasional expedition with her father. For Sarah, part of the attraction of Windermere was probably the company of her sister, Elizabeth Todhunter, whose husband managed Luskintyre, three kilometres away on the opposite bank of the Hunter River but visible from Windermere. Covering 2,000 acres (800 hectares), Luskintyre had a good house and outbuildings set in lightly timbered grass lands. Both estates had been cleared since the late 1820s and the arable parts were farmed by tenants who grew wheat and lucerne. Wentworth developed a 30 acre (12 hectare) vineyard at Windermere which he staffed with German vignerons.[35]

The depression of the early 1840s was slow to affect Wentworth. In partnership with T.M.W. Winder and Charles Nott, he opened a boiling down works at Windermere in 1844. As well as his own sheep, animals of his neighbours were slaughtered and rendered into tallow. Though the smells and smoke from the works, "the most extensive and complete in the colony", disturbed the beauty of Windermere, boiling down provided Wentworth with a substitute income when sheep prices were low. Windermere butter also provided a cash income, £209 in 1844 and £186 in 1845, but Wentworth's most stable source of cash was rental payments from his Sydney properties. Rental income from 31 city properties in 1836 was £1,195. Despite the depression, rents brought in £1,527 on 26 Sydney properties in 1844 and £1,248, from 22 properties, in 1845. These funds were drawn on by Sarah and the children for shopping, domestic needs and property repairs.[36]

During the 1830s Wentworth had invested heavily in land and stock. His major creditor was T.M.W. Winder, from whom he had borrowed £24,710 in 1836 for Windermere. All but £2,000 had been repaid by 1849, the year when Wentworth was most tightly pressed for cash. During the depression years he expanded, borrowing to take advantage of low prices and the liquidity crises of colonists with less credit than himself. By 1851 he had mortgages for about £60,000. Wentworth maintained his own liquidity

Above left: Thomasine [Timmie] Fisher (nee Wentworth) (1825-1913). *Private Collection.*
Above right: William Charles Wentworth junior (1827-1859). *Vaucluse House Collection.*

through a series of mortgages and land sales, especially in 1845 and 1847 when his land transactions in each year exceeded £52,000.

These financial arrangements had implications for Sarah. Under English common law a widow was entitled to one-third of the freehold lands of her husband as compensation for her loss of property rights on her marriage. Dower obligations were easily avoided by landowners. In New South Wales dower was gradually restricted to women married before 1837 and Wentworth himself proposed a bill in 1850 which restricted the right of dower to wives resident in the colony.[37] Following the marriage of their eldest daughter in 1844 and probably in view of the uncertain financial climate of the 1840s, Wentworth established a trust fund to protect Sarah's dower. A deed of 3 September 1845 named their son-in-law, T.J. Fisher, as Sarah's trustee and compelled Wentworth to pay part of any income raised by sale or mortgage of his land into a trust fund for Sarah's use on his death or bankruptcy. The proportion from any transaction varied from 5 to 10 per cent, significantly less than the traditional one-third. Fisher refused to act as trustee and the funds were not secured until the mid-1850s, by which time Sarah had secured dower of £24,416 on lands sold by her husband since 1845. In February 1853, on the eve of her departure for England, she surrendered her right to dower in Wentworth's remaining land, presumably to enable him to speed up the settlement of his affairs during her absence, since her signature was required to release dower on each land sale.[38]

In February 1844 their eldest son, Willie, had boarded the *Palestine* bound for England to continue his education.[39] It was a journey most sons of the wealthier colonial families had to endure but it was a hard parting for Sarah. In later years she never forgave herself for letting him go, blaming years of loneliness for his tragic end and she became excessively protective of Fitz and D'Arcy, refusing to leave them alone in England for their schooling.

Wentworth had unrealistically high expectations for Willie, who was to train as a lawyer despite hearing and eye-sight difficulties that would make it unlikely he could ever practise. The boy was told to study hard and always strive to be first. Success was essential, for upon Willie's shoulders could rest the eventual support of the family. The depression of the 1840s and the devaluation of property had shaken his father's confidence in his long-term prosperity. Wentworth, no doubt remembering his own youth, particularly cautioned Willie against the "thoughtless and profligate set" so often found in the universities and warned him to avoid John Wentworth (his father's half-brother), who was at Cambridge enjoying a life of dissipation.[40] Willie was sent to a private tutor, a clergyman, to study for a year or two before entering Trinity College, Cambridge. In November 1846 Wentworth's political opponent, Robert Lowe, wrote to an Oxford colleague seeking a tutor for Wentworth's son, a "restive colt." It was difficult for "a parent who is quite unable, from the immense distance and the pressure of business, to come to. England himself, and has no one to whom to entrust a matter of so much difficulty."[41]

Though Wentworth personally had little time for established religion, he permitted Sarah to arrange religious instruction for their daughters. Opinions about Sarah's immorality made it especially important that she and her daughters be seen to conform in church attendance. For 72 shillings a year, they rented a pew at fashionable St James's Church of England and Sarah, her sister-in-law Eliza, her daughters and niece Mary Todhunter attended on Sundays. It was an opportunity to display their finery and, in a limited way, mix in colonial society. Here the girls were confirmed and here, after a morning service in 1844, Sarah was congratulated on her daughter Timmie's marriage by Sydney fashionables such as the Shadforths and the Milfords.[42]

Acquaintances from church, her husband's business associates and the families of friends of her children were the source of most of Sarah's social contacts outside her own family. Frequent house guests at Vaucluse were the Moriarty, Milford and Cape families. Lydia Moriarty, one of six daughters of

South Head Lighthouse, near Vaucluse, a favourite venue for Wentworth family picnics. Lithograph after Robert Russell in J.G. Austin *A Series of Lithographic Views of Sydney and its Environs*, Sydney, 1836. *Mitchell Library.*

port master M.M. Moriarty, was a friend of Fanny's, as was Eliza Milford, a daughter of S.F. Milford, a legal officer who, like Moriarty, had arrived in the colony at the time Wentworth entered the Legislative Council. Mrs Jane Cape and her children and the family of Wentworth's legal associate, C.H. Chambers, joined in picnics Sarah arranged at South Head lighthouse through her friendship with Jane Siddins, wife of the lighthouse keeper.[43]

Sarah Wentworth (1805-1880).
Watercolour and pencil by William Nicholas c.1852.
Private Collection.

CHAPTER 4

Damned Whore

FAMILY AND HOME were the centre of many women's lives but for Sarah Wentworth, her world was confined to these activities not by choice but by colonial social conventions. One commentator on the period has noted that

> as the wife's functions increased and she undertook the moral guidance and elementary education of the children, it was seen as essential that she conform to bourgeois moral standards. So, although a woman characterised as a Damned Whore could marry and raise children, the stigma of the stereotype would brand her forever, in the eyes of society if not her husband, and her fitness for performing these functions would always be called into question.[1]

In colonial New South Wales social distinctions between a respectable free élite and the mass of tradesmen and convict labourers were matters of great controversy. The upper ranks of colonial society were drawn from government and military officials and their families, together with a few colonists who had arrived as free settlers and maintained a wealthy and morally respectable presence. From the earliest years of settlement, the social élite had been defined as those who received invitations to the governor's levees and balls. When a governor invited the "wrong" people, such as when Macquarie admitted emancipists to Government House society, a storm broke out. Among the women, gentility was increasingly equated with sexual respectability.

In such a world Sarah Wentworth was an outcast. Colonial born, illegitimate and the daughter of twice convicted parents, her birth could have been overlooked had her moral behaviour been without blemish. By cohabiting with Wentworth and bearing his children before their marriage, she offended the moral standards of the colonial élite. For this, she was never forgiven and she carried the stigma of "damned whore" until her death. She was snubbed by those who considered themselves her superiors, and any moral failings of her family served only to emphasise her failure as an example to them. Her husband was powerless to protect her from such judgements and, despite his financial and political success, the Wentworth family were social outcasts. This exclusion contributed significantly to their decision to bring up their children in England.

Wentworth's violent political and personal attacks on Governor Darling meant that he was excluded from functions at Government House in the 1820s and his criticism of the colonial secretary, Alexander Macleay, ensured his rejection by the official and cultural élite. A new governor, Sir Richard Bourke, arrived in Sydney in December 1831 but his wife was seriously ill and died six months later. Eliza Darling considered that this was fortuitous as it prevented Bourke from holding a ball to celebrate the King's Birthday to which he had invited 500 people including

> Mr and Mrs *Wentworth*...and some others, who must have been asked...simply because they were *radicals*, for they had not any *pretensions* to being in that Class of Society....It was thought people ought to be born and educated as gentlefolks, before they should be admitted to Government House — Mr Wentworth *himself* as a Barrister, educated at Oxford, might certainly have been asked, but his *Wife*, having lived with him for years, has only recently become his wife, and when we *left*, used to sit at a *Stall* selling *Beef*, in consequence of the very low price of Cattle and Mr Wentworth having so many Thousands, he had set up a Butcher's Shop.[2]

Bourke and Wentworth shared a similar political outlook and Bourke accepted him as a man of wealth and ability. Wentworth, though not Sarah, was invited to stay at Government House, Parramatta for a few days in early 1833. In December 1835 Bourke included Wentworth's name among those whom he considered suitable to be nominated as members of the Legislative Council and a month later commissioned Wentworth as a justice of the peace.[3] In February 1836 Bourke visited Vaucluse where he probably met Sarah. This visit aroused much speculation and Wentworth felt compelled to issue a statement to the press stressing that the governor had not dined at Vaucluse but merely inspected extensions to the house. Suspicion that the governor shared a meal with a "damned whore" like Sarah Wentworth caused outrage. Speculation about the close relationship between Bourke and Wentworth fuelled rumours that Wentworth, the colony's leading barrister, might be raised to the bench to fill the vacancy created when the Chief Justice went to England.[4]

Despite Wentworth's standing with Bourke, Sarah probably did not attend social events at Government House. Colonial society had been quick to censure the governor's conduct in countenancing women with disreputable associations. In autumn 1836 Bourke invited a daughter of Sir John Jamison of Regentville to a private party at Government House. Jamison, a political colleague of Wentworth, was unmarried. Harriet Jamison did not attend the function because the ladies of the colony, led by Mrs Manning and Mrs Plunkett, the wives of senior members of the legal profession, refused to meet her. Undaunted, Bourke gave Harriet away at her wedding the following year.[5]

Lady Franklin, wife of the lieutenant governor of Van Diemen's Land, visited Sydney in 1839. She was acquainted with Major D'Arcy Wentworth and his wife who lived near Launceston, and so she took particular note of the Sydney Wentworths. William she described as a man of large property, considerable talent and a great radical who had lived with a lady whom he later married. Sarah, his wife, was "very handsome, lady like and amiable, but of course not visited."[6] A rigid formula of social etiquette on visiting by the late 1830s enabled the gentry to keep undesirable people at a distance. The ladies of the social élite dominated philanthropic work, controlling the committees to which membership was offered by invitation only. This effectively excluded women such as Sarah Wentworth from involvement in institutional charity work.[7]

Sarah's reputation as a "fallen woman" limited her role as a political hostess who could enhance her husband's career through social gatherings. Her house guests at Vaucluse were mainly family, a few of the intellectual élite, such as the Cape family, legal colleagues, especially the Chambers family, and government officials who had arrived in the early 1840s, such as the Moriartys and the Milfords, who did not know of or were indifferent to her circumstances but recognised the strength of Wentworth's personality and power.

As a mother, Sarah's role was to find suitable husbands for her daughters. Her exclusion from society meant that she could not take the girls to private parties where they would meet young men and women from the more respectable families. Her sister-in-law, Eliza Macpherson Wentworth, had been popular in Sydney society when she lived there in the late 1820s. Lady Franklin mistakenly assumed that Major Wentworth and his wife lived in Van Diemen's Land because Eliza Wentworth was embarrassed by her father-in-law's background as a highwayman and his brood of illegitimate children. On the contrary, Eliza Wentworth was very fond of her nieces and while living in Sydney in the early 1840s introduced 17-year-old Thomasine into colonial society in a way that her mother could not, even taking her to musical evenings at Government House where Lady Gipps complimented Timmie on her musical talents.[8]

Thomasine's marriage to T.J. Fisher in 1844 revealed the strength of colonial prejudice against mixing with the Wentworth family. Thomas John Fisher arrived in Sydney aboard the *Lady Kennaway* in October 1841. A lawyer in his late twenties, his mother was a sister of Robert Wardell and joint heiress to Wardell's estate, of which Wentworth was executor. Seven years after Wardell's murder, the estate had not been settled and Fisher had

Sarah Wentworth (left) and her daughter Thomasine [Timmie] *(right)* by Charles Abrahams, c.1844. It was unusual to commission portrait busts of women in the colony at that time. *Vaucluse House Collection.*

been sent out by the family to finalise their affairs. He was admitted as a barrister before the Supreme Court on 18 October 1841 and soon established himself among the Sydney legal fraternity.[9] A colleague, Thomas Callaghan, commented in May 1842 that Fisher had

> very good abilities and somewhat too good an opinion of them yet at least he does not sufficiently conceal his own estimate of his own acquirements but he is a young man of gentlemanly feeling and of reserved habits....we are thrown a good deal together in this dull dreary *metropolis*. Fisher has been well trained for the Bar or rather for the law and there can be no doubt of his acquiring a good practice[10]

Fisher was soon drawn into Wentworth's circle of influence. In late 1842 Wentworth suggested that Fisher stand at the forthcoming election for the Bathurst electorate where Wentworth owned a great deal of property. Fisher declined, pleading pressure of his legal work. A few months later he proposed to 18-year-old Thomasine. Though strongly attracted to Fisher who made "everything appear a dream to me", Timmie refused his offer.

Wentworth was not opposed to the match and extended a casual invitation to Fisher to dine with the family but Fisher pleaded a prior engagement. Yet in mid-1843 he seconded Wentworth's nomination as a candidate for Sydney in the forthcoming election, thereby arousing some antagonism.[11]

In January 1844 the *Sydney Morning Herald* announced the marriage of Thomasine, eldest daughter of W.C. Wentworth, member of the Legislative Council and barrister at law, to Thomas John Fisher, barrister at law and nephew of the late Dr Robert Wardell of Petersham. They were married by licence, with the consent of the bride's father as Thomasine was under age. Witnesses to the ceremony were W.C. Wentworth of Vaucluse, Thomasine's cousin, Mary Todhunter of Luskintyre, and her aunt, Elizabeth Wentworth, wife of Major D'Arcy Wentworth.[12] In the congregation were her mother and Dr a'Beckett, a friend of Fisher's who consoled Sarah with the trite comment that she was not losing her child but gaining a son. Shortly before the marriage, Wentworth commissioned the sculptor Charles Abrahams to execute a bust of Timmie. On her marriage, Wentworth gave her land valued at £7,000 at Milk Beach, Vaucluse, at Macquarie and Goulburn Streets and four farms totalling 357 acres (145 hectares) at Queen Charlotte Vale, Bathurst. Her uncle, D'Arcy Wentworth, was appointed as trustee. The properties were to be retained for five years, with Wentworth reserving the first option to purchase if the land was offered for sale. All rents and profits were assigned to Thomasine and the land was to be inherited by her children, failing whom it would revert to her father.[13]

Immediately after the wedding Fisher broke off social contact with his parents-in-law and forbade his wife to see her parents. This alienation lasted for 20 years. Fisher, torn between his desire for Thomasine and his fear that association with the Wentworth family would exclude him from colonial social life, had decided to marry Timmie but reject her family. He had discussed his fears with Eliza Macpherson Wentworth before the wedding but she thought he was referring to distant members of the family, such perhaps as Ann Lawes whom it was not expected that he would visit. She advised him that if the opinions of people such as the a'Beckett family worried him so much then he should not marry Timmie. It never occurred to her that Fisher meant to resolve his dilemma by separating Timmie from her parents. Eliza was shocked when, a month after the wedding, Fisher refused to let her visit Timmie at his country house at Tarban Creek.

> God knows! No one has a higher idea of the duty a wife owes to her
> husband.... and when his commands are lawful and just and cheerfully and most
> willingly should I obey them but when his commands infringe and are in direct
> opposition to those of my heavenly Father I would then most certainly...follow
> the dictates of my own conscience — I cannot comprehend how a husband — a

Christian husband could ask his wife to forsake her parents — parents too who have ever evinced the warmest, the most devoted affection for their child.[14]

Wentworth was defiant, convinced that Fisher would become ashamed of the estrangement and relax his prohibition. In the meantime, he reluctantly accepted it, commenting that "we do not consider it worth our while to court the little gentleman's acquaintance". Sarah managed to see her daughter a few times in the months following the wedding, meeting her at shops or at Wentworth's office. Her reaction to the crisis was more practical than her husband's defiance or her sister-in-law's distress, and she advised Timmie to send her laundry and any mending home to Vaucluse.[15]

A visitor to the Fisher household in July 1844 commented:

his wife is a mere child in her manners; she lent upon my shoulder as we were looking over some prints just as if I were her brother or had known her for years; she seems a girl of some strength of mind and intellect and plays and sings prettily. Fisher pets and fondles her desperately. He has some smartness but wants solidity and good taste very much.[16]

Sarah and William's first grandchild, Alice Fisher, was born at Fisher's chambers and residence in Castlereagh Street North on 27 October 1844. During her second pregnancy Timmie was ill and Fisher relaxed the ban on contact with her parents to allow her to go to her mother. William Wentworth Fisher was born at Vaucluse on 12 May 1846. He was ill for several weeks and was cared for by Sarah and Fanny. The reconciliation did not endure, however, beyond the emergency of Timmie's ill-health. Robert Fisher was born in August 1848 while his parents were living at Liverpool Street. Another son, Donnelly Fisher, was born at their Parramatta River residence, near Gladesville, in August 1850.[17]

Part of the difficulty in settling the Wardell estate lay in Wardell's failure to complete his purchase of Petersham from Wentworth before his death. Wentworth finalised the sale of 295 acres (120 hectares) at Petersham to Fisher on behalf of Wardell's sisters for £2,950 in April 1848 but the estate remained unresolved as late as 1854, provoking further friction with Fisher.[18] Fisher's refusal to have any direct dealings with Sarah or William created other legal difficulties. As part of Timmie's marriage settlement, Wentworth had arranged for Fisher to become a trustee for Sarah's entitlements to dower. Fisher refused to act and neglected the trust provisions. Eventually, in May 1848, Sarah agreed to replace Fisher with Robert Towns, Wentworth's brother-in-law, and Robert Allen Hunt, her own brother-in-law. In July 1848 her other brother-in-law, Richard Hill, replaced Towns as trustee.[19]

The social disaster and hypocrisy surrounding Timmie's marriage warned the Wentworths that greater care would be needed to introduce Fanny, their next daughter, into society. This time they would ensure that her background and family were accepted by her suitors. In mid-1844 a stunning drawing room was built at Vaucluse. It was designed to attract suitors to entertainments in the Wentworth family home, obviating the need for Sarah and her daughters to attend more public venues. On 23 February 1847, aged 18, Fanny Wentworth married squatter John Reeve of Tarra Villa, Gippsland, at St James's church with her father's consent. The witnesses were W. C. Wentworth and Eliza M. Milford, daughter of the Master in Equity and Fanny's friend.[20]

A widower many years Fanny's senior, John Reeve (c.1804-1875) came from a landed family of Lowestoft, a Suffolk coastal town. Arriving in Sydney in 1841, he took ship for Port Phillip and Gippsland. W. C. Wentworth was a fellow passenger. Reeve took up Tarra Villa, Gippsland in 1841 and prospered as a squatter. He had two stations on the La Trobe River: Snake's Ridge, which he held from March 1842 to 1849, was about 60,000 acres (24,000 hectares) on which he ran 1,200 cattle and 25,000 sheep; and Scarne, taken up in August 1847, was 7,680 acres (3,000 hectares) on which he ran cattle. Reeve also invested in land in Sydney, Moreton Bay and Melbourne. On one of his frequent trips to Sydney, he met and later married Fanny. For her marriage portion, William settled on Fanny four allotments in Melbourne, valued at £8,000, and appointed Samuel Raymond and Robert Towns as her trustees. After her marriage Fanny lived at Tarra Villa in Gippsland but in December 1850 Reeve purchased 14 acres (5.5 hectares) of Vaucluse from his father-in-law and commissioned architect John Frederick Hilly to build their home, Greycliffe.[21]

The year 1847 was also memorable for the Wentworths in a less pleasant sense. Sir Charles FitzRoy had arrived as the new governor of New South Wales on 3 August 1846 and Lady Mary FitzRoy gave her first party three weeks later. In the months that followed she held dances every week and many attended her parties who had avoided Government House functions because of political differences with Governor Gipps. Yet before long there were rumblings of discontent about the names that appeared on Lady Mary's guest list. It was rumoured that she was "surrounded by a bad clique of ancient dames, and it is feared that those same elderlies will lead her Ladyship astray".[22]

The Queen's Birthday Ball was usually held in May but the 1847 celebrations were postponed until 22 June because George FitzRoy, the governor's son and private secretary, broke his leg in early May. The delay allowed time for close scrutiny of the guest list. In the eyes of both the Sydney press and the colonial élite too many people of "doubtful reputation" had received invitations to the ball.[23] A few individuals became the objects

Greycliffe on the Vaucluse Estate, built c.1850 by architect J.F. Hilly for Fanny and John Reeve. Pencil sketch by Conrad Martens. *Mitchell Library.*

of specific criticism. Though not named in the press, it was widely known that one of the targets of the vicious campaign that followed was Sarah Wentworth. Elizabeth Macarthur commented that many had refused to attend the ball because Sarah Wentworth and a few others had been invited.

> the Chief Justice has ventured to object to some persons invited to Govt House — I believe there are two others that find fault but have not given publicity to their opinions — the Ladies have taken umbridge by the introduction of Mrs Wentworth and one or two others[24]

Mrs Macarthur's use of "introduction" suggests that Sarah had not previously appeared at public vice-regal affairs. Now in her early forties, perhaps one of the "ancient dames" close to Lady Mary FitzRoy, Sarah was the wife of the colony's most prominent politician and wealthiest pastoralist. With her two eldest daughters married and her sister-in-law living again in Van Diemen's Land, Sarah probably hoped to establish herself in the new vice-regal circle so that she could introduce her younger daughters into society. Enduring the smear campaign that followed was an added pressure on Sarah's health as she was in the early months of pregnancy, carrying her tenth child.

Sarah Wentworth's invitation to Government House was the catalyst that activated a bitter social and moral debate which raged throughout May and June 1847. Colonial society was self-consciously aware that the convict past cast a shadow on the moral character of all colonists. There had always been a determined group anxious to be recognised as a moral élite and their attitudes and influence were as strong in the decade following the end of transportation as they had been in Macquarie's era. Vice-regal society had traditionally set the tone for the rest of colonial society and concern had been simmering from the first weeks of FitzRoy's administration that the new governor was lowering social standards. In the winter of 1847 the urge for colonial morality and respectability became linked with specific issues, such as the influence of the governor's aide-de-camp in issuing invitations to vice-regal parties and the order of precedence for officials on ceremonial occasions.

One observer of the debate was Colonel G.C. Mundy, a relative of FitzRoy.

> Except at the very earliest stage of my acquaintance with Sydney, its social atmosphere appeared to me singularly calm and placid. On that one occasion, indeed, it was convulsed in all its elements — from the representative of majesty to the printer's devils of the press — by a sudden and determined attempt to cause to be erased from the list of the 11 or 1200 occasional visitors at Government House the names of two or three persons far advanced in years and much esteemed by those who knew them, who in the somewhat lax infancy of the colony had, it was said, taken on themselves parental responsibilities without due regard to ritual; but who had long since submitted to its yoke, and had reared for their adopted country one or two generations of excellent and estimable citizens....such was the social uproar, such the disunion, ill-blood and recrimination, that, at first, I feared that in venturing to Sydney I had stumbled into some hot bed of active and fearful dissipation!...I was as much amused as I was able to be with a circumstance involving as much cruelty as absurdity; and I could not but congratulate the community upon the fact, that, in order to find a flaw in its immaculateness, it had been necessary to rake up again to the surface frailties that had been forgotten and had, as it were, become fossilized by the lapse of ages! As far as I know, this was the only serious crusade against character that occured in my time.[25]

Leading the newspaper campaign was the *Atlas*, a paper launched in 1844

Ball at Government House. *Illustrated Sydney News*, 1853.
State Library of New South Wales.

with backing from pastoralists and squatters, including W.C. Wentworth. The editor from May 1845 to August 1847 was James Martin, journalist, lawyer and sometime political protégé of Wentworth. Regular contributors included barristers Robert Lowe and Archibald Michie. Identified with the ambitions of the colonial-born youths, though he had arrived in the colony as a baby, Martin's character included a strong element of snobbery. He had attacked the social and land policies of Gipps and soon focused on the private life of the new governor.

A few weeks after FitzRoy's arrival, the *Atlas* reminisced that Gipps, through his Squatting Acts and his invitations to Government House, had tried to "level all social distinctions, and reduce to the same degradation, the educated and the ignorant, the elegant and the vulgar, the honest and the dishonest, the moral and the depraved". Anticipating that with Gipps's departure, moral standards would improve, the *Atlas* deplored the character of recent guests at Government House and warned FitzRoy against imitating the morals of his profligate ancestor, Charles II. Because of their rank, Sir Charles and Lady Mary Fitzroy could mix with the immoral without fear that their taste and personal morality were suspect; however, everyone would assume the worst of colonists who associated with the immoral.[26]

The *Atlas* returned to this theme in November 1846, criticising FitzRoy for visiting the homes of certain disreputable people and inviting them to his own table, thereby forcing contact between the pure and the wicked. No longer governor of an uneducated and immoral West Indian colony, in New South Wales FitzRoy might daily meet his equals in social standing and his superiors in ability and education and they would not tolerate being treated with such contempt. In particular, the colonists demanded the exclusion of immoral women to "preserve our wives and daughters safe from the contagion which they might spread."[27]

FitzRoy's aide-de-camp, Edward Merewether, had served as Gipps's aide since 1842 and he was blamed for his advice to the governor on whom to invite to vice-regal functions. Merewether was transferred to the settlement in North Australia in December 1846 and Lieutenant Charles C. Master of the 58th Regiment became responsible for protocol at Government House. When the guest list for the 1847 Queen's Birthday Ball was made known, the *Atlas* demanded the removal of the new aide-de-camp.[28]

Other Sydney papers entered the debate. Editorials supporting the *Atlas* appeared in the *Herald* and the *Australian*. Word had spread that two judges of the Supreme Court had refused to visit Government House. The chief justice, Sir Alfred Stephen, had been knighted in 1846. He was very proud of his honours and was deeply offended in April 1847 to learn that the Colonial Office had decreed that the Church of England Bishop of Australia should take precedence over the judges at official functions. Stephen argued that it was important politically, judicially and morally that the judges be seen to be men of high social standing and rank. By refusing to meet the governor's guests the judges made a political statement in defence of their moral and social superiority.[29]

The *Herald* argued that no-one should have to meet at Government House people who were never invited to other respectable family homes:

> Damaged female characters...albeit they had been completely and clerically repaired, should be uncompromisingly shut out.... Whenever a woman falls, she falls for ever.... She becomes as it were socially dead. Her punishment is indeed worse than death.... If compromise and distinction between particular cases were allowed, a door would remain open.... A few individual instances of hardship may occur but a much greater number are prevented.... There should be no statute of limitations enacted for the relief of female error. Should the reader have a wife or sister, he would not desire that she should be at any time

introduced to a reformed lady of easy virtue, however romantic, peculiar or pitiable her individual case.[30]

Sarah Wentworth, in the eyes of Sydney society, would always be a "lady of easy virtue". She should have no part in public life because she would contaminate young and innocent girls by her presence and her example. The attack cut deeper than the plight of the individual woman. "A mother's moral character was everything in the formation of the character of her children", thundered the *Herald*. By implication, Sarah's sins would be visited on her daughters. Their every action would be examined for signs of their mother's immorality.[31] The *Australian* repeated the *Herald's* editorial but recognised the injustice of blaming only the women.

> It is woman's own fault that her seducer is not alike degraded and despised. But, whilst women will welcome and wed the destroyers of their sex, whilst mothers will permit them to defile their dwellings, the scales of social justice will continue to be unevenly and iniquitously balanced.[32]

By mid-June 1847 the debate against immoral women had become specific. The chief justice and his legal associates formally protested to the governor against the invitation of three women to the Queen's Birthday Ball. The press, without naming the women, agreed that two of the women, one being Sarah Wentworth, were undoubtedly guilty of immoral behaviour but there was no evidence against the third. The critics did not condemn the current behaviour of these women, only their past, acknowledging that

> These ladies have been exemplary mothers for twenty years, and are visited by ladies moving in the best society. They are very highly esteemed in society generally, being considered patterns, as English matrons, in all that adorns the domestic hearth and the family circle. They have large families of well-educated sons and daughters; some of the latter married to gentlemen of rank and fortune.[33]

Under such pressure the women indicated to Lady Mary FitzRoy that they would withdraw from Government House functions and apologised for the scandal.[34]

The debate focused attention on so many domestic situations that the *Australian* eventually decided that, for the sake of the children and grand-children of the early settlers, prudence and charity should prevail and discussion of the past should be dropped. It reminded its readers that New South Wales in its first 40 years had few females, either convict or immigrant, who were suitable to form legitimate alliances with officers and gentlemen. Hobson's choice prevailed and many men who dreaded marriage with such women chose concubines instead of wives.[35]

Legislative Council of N.S.W. 6th June, 1844.
Watercolour by Jacob Janssen. *National Library of Australia.*

FitzRoy's ball in June 1847 was well attended. Everyone of standing was there so that the absentees — Chief Justice Alfred Stephen, Justice John Dickinson, Robert Lowe and Archibald Michie — were noticeable. FitzRoy addressed the guests, defending his right to dispense hospitality as he and his wife wished. However, social life under the FitzRoys came to an abrupt end a few months later when Lady Mary FitzRoy and Lieutenant Master were killed in a carriage accident at Parramatta on 7 December 1847.[36]

Life in the public arena had inured Wentworth to attack and, as a skilled public orator, he was master of riposte. He rarely acknowledged personal attacks on himself or his family but personal allusions became more common with elective government in 1842 and as the political struggles of the 1840s involved more diverse social groups. Earlier in 1847 Robert Lowe

53

had referred to Wentworth's father, sneering that becoming a squatter was the equivalent of turning highwayman. Attacks on Sarah Wentworth, the wife of a controversial political figure, were also an indirect way of attacking Wentworth, though the Queen's Birthday Ball debacle struck far deeper into colonial consciousness.

For Sarah, the controversy of 1847 led to her insistence that her younger daughters must be brought up in England. Timmie and Fanny were old enough to understand the accusations against their mother. By implication their own morality was suspect because they had been raised by an immoral woman. Their solution was to turn to religion, seeking respectability through good works. Timmie, concerned about the influence of her father's outspoken secularism on her younger sisters, urged her mother to ensure the girls received religious instruction. Sarah replied, a little tartly, that Timmie did not give her father sufficient credit for his concern for his children. He had told her to take care of the girls' religious upbringing. [37]

Willie had been unaware of his illegitimacy. Just as his father had learnt of D'Arcy Wentworth's arraignment as a highwayman through a public debate in 1819, so Willie learnt of the circumstances of his birth through the bitter controversy of 1847. Taunted by other colonial boys in England, he asked John Cox, his mother's half-brother, for details of the family background. Illegitimacy had financial implications of which Willie was probably ignorant. D'Arcy Wentworth's will was a confused document in which property inherited by his children reverted to his eldest son, W.C. Wentworth, and then in turn to his eldest son. This interpretation was challenged, and upheld, in *Wentworth* v. *Bath* in June 1848 and *Towns* v. *Addison* in September 1850. Legal documents drafted by Sarah Wentworth in November 1851 and by William Charles Wentworth in March 1854 refer to their second son, Fitzwilliam, as heir to any property reverting to W.C. Wentworth under his father's will. Willie, their eldest son, would inherit nothing through his grandfather's will. Sarah's allocation of her dower entitlements, though providing the usual support for her daughters and grandchildren, was structured primarily to provide an income for life for her eldest, but illegitimate, son. [38]

The humiliation of the winter of 1847 was pushed to the background as more pressing family matters intervened. On 10 January 1848 Sarah's tenth child, D'Arcy Bland Wentworth, was born. Wentworth was re-elected as a member of the Legislative Council in July 1848 but pleasure in political success and expanding family was overshadowed by financial problems: Windermere and Belltrees had to be vacated and let in late 1848. [39]

Wentworth was not alone in having weathered the earlier years of the depression only to experience cash flow difficulties in the late 1840s, difficulties which intensified with news of the Privy Council's decision on the affairs of the Bank of Australia, which had collapsed in 1843. Shareholders of the bank were required to repay an amount equal to the face value of their shares and the real estate assets were to be sold. Wentworth, a shareholder, was called upon for £3,200, not a large sum in view of his assets, yet he did not settle until late 1850, then offering a part cash payment and the balance in promissory notes payable over 18 months.[40]

Part of the property of the Bank of Australia was dispersed through the sale of lottery tickets in January 1849. A similar scheme was proposed to Wentworth, who was under pressure from some of his creditors. The *Sydney Morning Herald* of 2 February 1849 carried an announcement under the name of James Martin offering an equitable partition of some of Wentworth's land. Depressed prices meant that land sales would not raise adequate funds and so a lottery was advertised. Land valued at £20,000 in the centre of Sydney, suburban properties within a six mile (10 kilometre) radius of the city worth £10,000, agricultural land and pastoral stations with stock worth £30,000 would be the prize for the lucky winner. Twelve thousand tickets at £5 each would raise £60,000, the extent of Wentworth's mortgages. Justification for the lottery was that, relieved of the management burden of his extensive properties, Wentworth would be able to concentrate on politics.

The lottery invited public scrutiny of Wentworth's private affairs. Cynics who saw it as an arrogant attempt to dispose of properties not easily or quickly sold by more orthodox methods were probably right. If William and Sarah planned to take their children to England, rationalisation of their colonial assets was essential. Political commentators noted that Wentworth had never before pleaded lack of time to pursue his public interests. Perhaps it was a ruse to prevent the second Bank of Australia lottery. If so, it succeeded; the bank's lottery was cancelled and settlement of its affairs deferred until 1851. Wentworth's lottery was also cancelled, through the intervention of the attorney-general, in April 1849, though Wentworth did not recall the tickets or offer refunds until July.[41]

Coinciding with the anti-transportation meetings of early 1849, the financial difficulties of the "bullying, bellowing champion of the Few" found little sympathy with the more radical colonists. Satirist Charles Harpur taunted:

A Patriot? — He who has no sense nor heed
Of public ends beyond his own mere need!
Whose country's ruin to his public fear
Means only this — the loss of Windermere![42]

Representative government had meant that, more than ever, Sarah had to share her husband with his political ambitions for colonial self-government. "The love of my country has been the master passion of my life", said Wentworth in 1848, and Sarah accepted this.[43] No-one, whether friend or foe, denied the dominance of Wentworth's personality but, as her husband became increasingly isolated from the working class immigrants of his Sydney electorate, a critical press forced Sarah to see him through their eyes.

> That is he, that English-drover-looking old man, with the heavy, loose, drab coat, and the mass of grizzled hair....That is the senior member for Sydney, who, be his faults what they may — and they are like a brickfielder about him — has still the great honour of having been the first champion of Australian liberty. There is something of commanding ruin in the personal aspect of Mr Wentworth.....His ability in debate is perhaps greater than any other member. In his public speaking, there is an inexcusable slovenliness and disrespectful bearing, which would never be tolerated at all, if he did not possess superior intellect....there are times, when neither self-interest is at stake, nor blinding jealousies disturb him, which witness him rise to the stature of a giant over his compeers. Few have equal power with Mr Wentworth, to support their own or to demolish an opponent's arguments; and none can command more forcible and original language....The tones of his voice are discordant, and grating, sometimes running into a loud, harsh, impatient and decided drawl, especially so when he is thwarted in his personal aims....His action is inelegant and random, though often imparting emphasis to his assertions....Mr Wentworth is bordering on three score years; his personal appearance is tall and athletic, slightly stooping as from the pressure of time; his countenance is florid, and marked by courage and determination.[44]

Wentworth's financial situation received an unexpected boost when gold was discovered at Summer Hill Creek, near Orange, in February 1851. Summer Hill Creek ran through Wentworth's land at Frederick's Valley and gold was discovered on his land in mid-1851. Wentworth issued goldmining licences at 30 shillings a month to his tenants. A decade later the Wentworth gold field, known as Lucknow, became one of the richest fields in New South Wales. Political and social priorities also changed in the early 1850s. As Wentworth's alienation from the new urban population deepened, his old sparring partners became allies. The depth of this change was encapsulated in a dinner invitation. Wentworth invited James and Edward Macarthur to dine with his family at Vaucluse — and they accepted. On the last Sunday in September 1852 James Macarthur was introduced to Sarah Wentworth for the first time. He was impressed.

> The family are very quiet and nice looking — quite prepossessing in their appearance and Mrs W. is much more the Lady in manner and appearance than many who give themselves great airs of exclusiveness.[45]

Vaucluse in the late 1840s after the addition of the large drawing room.
Oil painting by G.E. Peacock. *Private Collection.*

Lunch was a family gathering with Fanny and her husband, John Reeve; Captain Towns, Wentworth's brother-in-law; Mr Hunt, Sarah's brother-in-law; family friends Dr Bland and Mr Nowlan and an English visitor, Mr Dundas, MP. A few days later James Macarthur and Wentworth visited the North Shore orchard of Sarah's brother-in-law, Richard Hill, a strong supporter of Macarthur.

Yet, for many others, the Wentworths remained social outcasts. T. S. Mort, whose great success as an auctioneer and industrialist lay in the future, commented of Wentworth in the early 1850s:

> I have never met him in society as he did not move in the same spheres as myself. Had he visited the principal families in the colony at that time I must have met him, as I exchanged visits with nearly the whole of them.[46]

The wealthier classes sent their sons to Europe to be educated but this was "always resorted to with great regret". Doubtless with his eldest son in mind, in 1849 Wentworth had been a member of the select committee that recommended that a university be established in Sydney. Fitzwilliam Wentworth passed his matriculation examinations for entry to the University of Sydney in October 1852 but classes offered at the new institution were, however, limited. Wentworth wanted him to attend university in England but Fitz was the most sickly of their children and it was unlikely that Sarah would send him alone to England.[47]

Their financial affairs had improved but with increased political activity connected with the Constitution Bill, it was a bad time for Wentworth to leave the colony. He suggested that Sarah take the children to England. At first she resisted, doubting that she could manage without him, but concern about Willie, whom she had not seen for nine years, overcame her fears:

> nothing would induse me to go without him if I only considered myself — but you must think how many years poor Willie has been left to himself and how uneasey I have been for fear he was terrified to do any act that might not be easey to [resolve?] Your Papa would not feel satisfied without arranging his concern so that he could feel safe in England — and he could not tell till next June so that he would not have any debts to trouble him — and he has some other act to do in Council he would not be pleased to finish his political career till he has brought some plan for general Education[48]

Sarah felt that she would be safe travelling at her age with her 20-year-old son as escort if they followed Wentworth's instructions. The decision made, practical needs kept Sarah's hands and mind busy. There were clothes to be made for the children, packing for the voyage and an indefinite stay abroad, as well as compiling inventories of items at Vaucluse to be stored or sold. Sarah, Fitzwilliam, the six youngest children and a companion/governess,

Miss Morris, sailed in February 1853 on the *Carnatic*. The decision to take the children to England marked the end of a settled home life for Sarah. From the date of her departure in 1853 until her death in 1880, Sarah rarely lived in one place for more than two years.

Vaucluse was stripped bare. Its contents, an assortment of elegant household furniture, a grand piano, silver, china, glassware, paintings, books, horses and carriages, were auctioned the month after Sarah sailed and the house was advertised to let. John Hosking took a three year lease from January 1854 at an annual rent of £400. Two years later he purchased neighbouring Milk Beach from Thomasine and her husband, extending his tenancy at Vaucluse until January 1858 while his home, Carrara, was built.[49]

Before she left, Sarah was anxious to have small portraits made of all the family, especially Timmie of whom she wanted two portraits, one for herself and another for Willie in England. William Nicholas, a miniaturist, depicted Sarah as a plain, almost severe-looking woman with dark hair kept neatly in place with a cap. Her face reflected a calm, quiet dignity and strength. Though Sarah hoped her husband would bring the portraits to England, Wentworth offered them to Timmie for safekeeping, together with a medallion of himself by Thomas Woolner. Fisher probably refused to hang the portraits and so they were left with the Hills.[50]

Wentworth remained behind in Sydney for a year, living in his town house on Church Hill. Here he and members of a select committee drafted the constitution for a self-governing New South Wales. Here also they considered a "bunyip aristocracy". Sarah was not in New South Wales to hear the debates about a hereditary upper house and the ambitions Wentworth held for their sons.

> No man, however, humble, can be debarred from aspiring to see his children educated and looking forward to achieve a position of rank and honour, and occupied in far higher pursuits than the money-making schemes of this filthy lucre-loving community....I have been taunted with entertaining a desire to be one of the hereditary legislators....but, admitting that I do, is it an improper object of ambition? Or am I to be denounced for cherishing the hope that some son of mine will succeed me in the councils of my country?[51]

The Constitution Bill was passed in December 1853 and sent to England. Colonial Secretary Deas Thomson and Wentworth followed to sponsor its passage through the British parliament. Wentworth's town house was leased for £600 per year in late February and he sailed for England aboard the *Chusan* in March 1854 accompanied, to Sarah's relief, by their daughter Fanny and her husband. Unable to find reliable managers, he had sold most of his pastoral stations. Farewell gatherings applauded him and raised funds

The departure of W.C. Wentworth for England in 1854.
Illustrated Sydney News, 1854. *State Library of New South Wales.*

for a statue, but Wentworth left with mixed feelings, remembering

> the rabid abuse to which every act of my public life for years past has been
> subjected. I cannot but feel that it required more than ordinary zeal and courage
> on the part of those who sided with me, to face such an ordeal as this.... what
> we have endured and accomplished together for the country, despite of all the
> vituperation and obliquy that have overtaken us, will be the most valued and
> agreeable retrospect of my public life. I trust I may arrive in London in time to
> hasten the ratification of our last great measure.[52]

A little cynical about the proposal for a statue of himself, he commented
that "I have not myself much taste in the fine arts but Mr Reeve has a good
deal" and would assist in the selection of a sculptor.[53]

CHAPTER 5

Colonist Abroad

SARAH AND THE CHILDREN arrived in London in June 1853. She had difficulty finding a house that suited her but eventually rented in Bayswater, a fashionable new area between Paddington station and Hyde Park. Southwick Crescent (now Hyde Park Crescent) was an expensive address. Nearby St John's Church was one of the focal points in the new estate.

Sarah's first concern was to see Willie. He had been admitted into the Middle Temple to study law in November 1849 but had withdrawn in January 1852. Knowing that Willie had been unhappy, Sarah was nevertheless shocked at the changes when she saw him again. Willie was very angry with her for not telling him about his grandfather, Francis Cox, and Sarah's own past. She confided to Timmie that she would not enquire too closely into his problems, confident that he had done nothing dishonourable but had merely been lonely. Under his mother's superintendence Willie, now in his mid-twenties, returned to his studies but Sarah doubted that he would complete his law degree. Disappointed by Willie's inability to settle to law, Wentworth gave him an annual allowance of £500 so that he could keep up the appearances of a gentleman and left him to pursue his hobby, chemistry.[1]

Fitzwilliam was enrolled at St John's College, Cambridge, in June 1853, though his father doubted that he had either the ability, application or health to complete his university studies. Sarah had more confidence in her second son.

> Fitz...is very steady....I am afraid Fitz must be the one to take some trouble off his father — therefore I do not think we shall have a lawyer in the family of the Wentworths[2]

Five-year old D'Arcy was enrolled in a day school in Bayswater. Singing and music masters, a French teacher and a governess were engaged for the five girls. Sarah was particularly anxious about the education of the eldest, Joody (Sarah Eleanor), who was 18. Her health was delicate, arising from complications of a fever she had caught in the colony. Joody learnt French in a class with other girls, struggling to keep up with them, but she enjoyed her music lessons.[3] The children quickly settled into London, enjoying it far more than home, where their peculiar social circumstances must have restricted their activities. They walked in the nearby gardens, went sightseeing and to concerts. Sarah was very impressed by a performance of Handel's Messiah. As family life had long been dominated by politics they went to see the Queen open parliament and Sarah thought Victoria looked more handsome than her pictures. Anxious that her grandchildren in the colony should be in style, Sarah dressed dolls in the latest children's fashions to send to Timmie.[4]

Despite these entertainments, Sarah did not enjoy her first winter in London. Homesick for Vaucluse, she eagerly welcomed spring with the return of green on the trees and cleaner air as winter fires were extinguished. Sarah missed her husband, promising Timmie that she would have her portrait done "after Papa arrives for I will be more settled then".[5] London, she recognised, offered her greater freedom than Sydney. It was a "place where women are treated better than any other place...for they are loved and cared for here".[6] Her comments were echoed by Fanny when she arrived in London a year later. Old enough to be aware of the ostracism of her mother in the colony, Fanny declared she would never go back to Sydney again.[7]

In May 1854 the children caught the measles and Sarah took them to Hastings for the sea air and open fields to run in, returning to London for her husband's arrival on 2 June 1854. This ended a 15 month separation, the longest of their marriage. The following weeks were wet and very cold. Fires burning morning and night did not prevent Wentworth succumbing to a severe cold.

> This climate...will not do for me, and I shall not be sorry when my period of exile expires. The greater part of my family, I believe, will be equally rejoiced to return. Those who have...lived in the colony do not know the many advantages they possess. They have only to come here to appreciate at once the immense superiority of climate and production which Australia enjoys over most other countries.[8]

With war in the Crimea, the constitutional politics of New South Wales had little priority for the British government. Wentworth met the Duke of Newcastle, the former secretary of state for the colonies, and dined privately with his successor, Sir George Grey. It was unlikely that the Australian constitutional legislation would be considered in the current session of parliament.[9]

November 1854 saw the Wentworths move to Brussels where they rented, for £200 a year, a furnished house at 19 Place Terrace. Brussels was an elegant city with a cathedral, botanical and zoological gardens, military barracks, a museum, picture gallery, fine shops and good schools. Living in Europe meant informal opportunities to make new acquaintances. With regular train services between Brussels and London, Wentworth could easily attend

Fanny Katherine Reeve (nee Wentworth) (1829-1893)
and her husband John Reeve (c.1804-1875). *Private Collection.*

political meetings in London while his daughters attended school in Brussels
as day pupils. Sarah believed that the best way for the girls to learn foreign
languages was to be with other young ladies who spoke no English.[10] Fanny
and John Reeve had offered to take Joody with them to Paris and Rome but
her father insisted that she stay at school in Brussels. Sarah was uncertain,
not wanting Joody to miss the benefits of foreign travel but fearful that
18-year-old Joody might form an unsuitable attachment away from her
parents' eyes. Undoubtedly Sarah was remembering the consequences of her
own youthful indiscretion. Fanny, in her opinion, did not have enough
worldly experience to be on her guard. Joody, therefore, would have to wait
a year until her parents could take her to Paris.[11]

Sarah and William made several visits to London to see their sons and
Sarah's sister, Maria Hunt, who was visiting England with her family.
Wentworth watched the progress of the Constitution Bill through parliament
and Sarah was pleased that he met so many influential people. The Wentworths
could not return to the colony until the lease of Vaucluse expired in 1857
but Wentworth was uncertain about their future. Several Australians were in
London and Wentworth soon became involved in lobbying for a direct mail
route through the Red Sea. He considered standing for parliament in Britain

but recognised that if he entered public life in England, their stay would become semi-permanent. He tried to persuade Sarah to live in the country where he could take up shooting. "But on this point she is inexorable. She says we came home to educate the girls and that they cannot be properly educated in the country which is probably true enough."[12]

Summer holidays saw the family, except D'Arcy who remained with friends in Brussels, at Aix-la-Chapelle for seven weeks. A short train journey from Brussels, the city, as Sarah noted, was known for its cloths, needles and the relics of Charlemagne but its attraction for her family was the sulphur baths. The girls, particularly Edith, had been ill and daily mineral baths were considered beneficial. From Aix-la-Chapelle they travelled to Switzerland, then Paris, returning to Brussels in October 1855. Here Wentworth left Sarah to arrange the family's move to Paris, where they were to spend the next year, while he went to England to farewell Deas Thomson who was returning to the colony. Sarah, too, would have liked to return to the colony "for after all I like it best" but the elder children preferred London and Europe because there was so much to interest them.[13]

They rented 44 Champs-Elysees, a comfortable house with a view of the Arc de Triomphe, for three months to see if they liked Paris. Didy (Eliza) who was 18 and Belle (Isabella), 15, attended a boarding school from Monday to Saturday and the younger girls, Laura and Edith, went to a day school in the Champs-Elysees. Edith, the youngest, was nearly 11 and Sarah thought the next two years of her education especially important. School work was harder in Paris than in Brussels. Joody, who was ill, was taught at home. Sarah enjoyed the bustle of Paris, though she did not like French servants and engaged English ones. In Paris she had several friends and acquaintances, like Mrs McIntosh, a sister of Eliza Wentworth, and William Macarthur, who was visiting Paris as a colonial commissioner for the Paris exhibition. His apartment was not far from the Wentworths and he became a regular visitor to their family dinners.[14]

Willie and Fitz joined their parents in Paris. Fitz had spent only a year at Cambridge. Probably like Alexander Oliver, a student from the University of Sydney, he felt lost at the larger universities in Britain. At Sydney there were 30 undergraduates; at Oxford there were 1,500. Moreover, many of the English students snubbed the Australians as rich, vulgar and ignorant.[15] Willie, however, had at last settled down to his legal studies, having formed an attachment to Amelia Hunt, his aunt's step-daughter. Sarah was content with the relationship, commenting that Amelia was old enough to know her own mind. "Amelia is very amiable and well principled — she would not be disagreeable in any way — perfectly lady like and he might be caught by an artful woman for he is still the same...as he was when a boy." Sarah still

Paris in the 1850s. The Bois de Boulogne.
Illustrated London News, 1856.

doubted that Willie would become a lawyer as his poor eyesight made studying difficult. Her eldest son had "great ability and a high sense of honor but odd ways".[16]

In mid-1856 the Wentworths returned to England. Sarah had finally agreed to her husband's wish to live in the country, though she thought it would prove very expensive, not only with rents but additional expenses because "you must entertain to be cheerful — for it is a dull life in a strange country".[17] They rented Deering House at Great Malvern in Worcestershire. Wentworth and John Reeve also rented the shooting over 3,000 acres (1,200 hectares) of the Duke of Marlborough's estate at Charlbury in Oxfordshire. Less than two and a half hours from London by train, it was more convenient to entertain their political and business friends than distant Worcestershire. Here William Macarthur joined them for a few days shooting partridge, hares and pheasants.[18] D'Arcy and Eliza Wentworth, recently arrived from Tasmania, joined Sarah at Great Malvern in mid-1856. Fanny and John

Reeve, who had bought a house at Rutland Gate in Knightsbridge, were visiting Sarah in August 1856 with their first child, five-month-old Arthur, when the baby died.

The death of their grandson was the start of a cycle of ill-health and death. Sarah herself usually enjoyed good health, her only problem a recurrent liver complaint that troubled her again in mid-1856 but "they say I am looking better". In October 1856 16-year-old Belle became seriously ill. Wentworth consulted specialists in London but there was no cure for the debilitating illness, a type of gastric fever, and Belle died within a few weeks. Sarah and William were distraught — she was the first of their children to die — and they fled from the unhappy associations of Great Malvern.[19] Sarah could not bear to let her other children out of her sight. Eight-year-old D'Arcy had been away at school but was brought home and sent to a day school, Hyde Park College. The Wentworths rented a house nearby at 57 Cleveland Square, Hyde Park. Laura and Edith were sent to a day school, Sarah justifying this choice rather than a boarding college with the comment that she could more easily watch their progress. Wentworth also had been ill in 1856 and, following Belle's death, he succumbed to a serious bout of influenza. A regular visitor during his illness was William Macarthur who commented that "age and hard living are beginning to tell heavily upon him".[20]

Joody's health deteriorated too. Sarah, unable to cope with her sick husband and the other children, sent her to stay with Fanny because Reeve was the only one able to persuade Joody to obey the doctors and take the medicine that she hated. Sarah worried that Joody, like Belle, would die. Fitzwilliam had returned to Cambridge but lung problems from mid-1856 had hindered his studies and delayed his entry to the Middle Temple to study law. Restricted to drinking cold water and taking cold baths, by July 1857 Fitzwilliam was dangerously ill from fever and debility.[21] Summer holidays found Sarah juggling health cures for the family. Her husband, Joody and D'Arcy were sent under the care of 19-year-old Didy to Kissengen, near Munich in Germany, to take the waters. Laura and Edith spent their holidays with their Aunt Eliza at Eastbourne, then went off to a boarding school. For Willie and Fitz, bathing at the seaside improved their health. Willie was working in a legal office but spending his leisure hours on chemistry experiments and Sarah feared his nervous system would collapse under the strain.[22]

Sarah, meanwhile, stayed alone in a hotel in London. Their lease at Cleveland Square had ended so she packed up the house and arranged for the storage of their belongings. She was to join her husband in Europe but before leaving London she wanted to see Timmie who had recently arrived

Isabella Christiana [Belle] Wentworth (1840-1856)
Watercolour possibly by William Nicholas, c.1852. *Private Collection.*

in England. The Fishers had sailed from Sydney in January 1856 to tour Europe and then settle in England. Eliza Wentworth hoped that away from the prying eyes and prattling tongues of Sydney, Timmie might be reunited with her parents but this was not to be. Fisher had a stormy encounter with Sarah in Covent Garden Market in mid-August 1857 during a meeting Sarah had arranged with Timmie. Sarah hoped for another opportunity to see her daughter "but if it should cause you any anger do not come for I see you have much to contend with."[23]

Accompanied by Fitz, who had to travel by easy stages, Sarah rejoined her husband in Kissengen for a tour of Europe. In Vienna by October 1857 her mind was awhirl with the places she had seen. She liked the Tyrol but preferred the scenery in Switzerland and was looking forward to Venice. Her pleasures, however, were overshadowed by the difficulties of travelling with sick children. Their intention was to find a warm place for the winter, possibly the south of France or Palermo in Sicily. They remained some weeks in Vienna because Joody was not strong enough to travel. By December they were in Corfu, off the coast of Greece. Here Wentworth and D'Arcy left them, D'Arcy to return to school and his father recalled to London by his lawyers. Fitz and Joody were both desperately ill and Didy remained with Sarah and her companion, Miss Morris, on Corfu, intending to continue to Sicily when the invalids were well enough to travel.

Wentworth wrote to Sarah from London, reassuring her that the children and himself had plenty of warm clothing, that D'Arcy was settled at school and Laura and Edith would spend their Christmas holidays with Fanny, then go to Brighton or the Isle of Wight with their uncle and aunt. Willie had lodgings in Norfolk Street, opposite Timmie. Wentworth wanted to see her for Christmas but "I dare not call on her for fear of making things unpleasant with Fisher." Fisher had permitted Timmie to visit Fanny who reassured her father that Timmie was well.[24]

On Corfu Joody's health deteriorated. The regimental surgeon pronounced her case hopeless, her lungs quite gone and her death imminent. She died on 23 December 1857, aged 22. A simple tablet marked the grave of Sarah Eleanor, third daughter of W.C. Wentworth and his wife, Sarah, of Vaucluse, Australia. Sarah anticipated Wentworth's instructions and buried her in a lead casket so that the remains could one day be returned to Australia. The authorities on Corfu, especially the High Commissioner of the Ionian Islands, Sir John Young, were sympathetic and obliging.[25] Sarah returned to London, leaving Fitz and Didy to spend the winter with Miss Morris in Italy. By February 1858 she had taken accommodation at 39 Jermyn Street. The lease of Vaucluse had expired and the Wentworths planned to return to the colony, settle their affairs, then establish a permanent home in England. The

Sarah Eleanor [Joody] Wentworth (1835-1857)
Portrait in oils by Thomas Gooderson. *Vaucluse House Collection*

thought of Vaucluse depressed Sarah, bringing back memories of happier days. Though Joody's death was not sudden like Belle's, Sarah had nursed her longer and felt her loss deeply.

In February 1858 the Privy Council handed down its decision in the case of *Towns* v. *Wentworth*. Wentworth's half-brothers and sisters, at the instigation of Robert Towns, had challenged D'Arcy Wentworth's will, which had provided that, if any of his children died without issue, the landed property would revert to the eldest child then living. George and John Wentworth had sold their estates to their brother-in-law, Robert Towns, but died without issue. As the eldest living son, W.C. Wentworth was entitled to the property of his deceased younger brothers and this was supported by the New South Wales Supreme Court. Towns appealed and the case was sent to England in July 1856. Interpretation of D'Arcy Wentworth's will was eventually determined by the Privy Council, which upheld the decision of the colonial court in favour of W.C. Wentworth.[26] With the law case settled, Sarah and William toured Europe in the spring of 1858, visiting Paris, Rome (for Wentworth to sit for his statue by Pietro Tenerani), Florence, Naples and Vienna. In Rome they also met the Australian artist Adelaide Ironside.

Their plans to return to New South Wales in 1858 were abandoned when Willie became seriously ill. Sarah and William had been pleased with his progress since he had met Amelia Hunt. Her father would not consider Willie as a future son-in-law unless he completed his legal studies and practised law for at least three months. In October 1855 Willie was re-admitted to the Middle Temple and was called to the Bar on 7 June 1858. Willie's confidant was his older sister, Timmie, who forwarded his letters to. Amelia because Maria Hunt had said that she would rather see her step-daughter dead than married to Willie Wentworth. In London, the Fishers lived opposite Willie but Thomas Fisher forbade visits. Brother and sister corresponded and arranged an occasional secret meeting. Willie wanted to go to New South Wales, marry Amelia, then practise law. As his failing eyesight might prevent him practising, the £500 a year allowance from his father would be sufficient to support a wife until he found suitable employment. Wentworth vigorously opposed Willie's marriage before he had completed his law studies, but Willie hoped that Timmie would persuade Sarah to convince his father to change his mind. He doubted that his mother, unless pushed by Timmie, would confront his father on this issue. Conscious that neither the Hunts nor his parents had much confidence in him, Willie hoped that success with his chemistry experiments would impress them, but he was depressed by forebodings that something would prevent him seeing Amelia again.[27]

Sarah was back in London by July 1858 and rented a house for three months at 21 Holles Street, Cavendish Square. By September she had moved

Thomasine [Timmie] Fisher (nee Wentworth) (1825-1913) and her husband
Thomas John Fisher (c.1813-1875). *Vaucluse House Collection.*

to a less elegant address, 4 Loudoun Road, St Johns Wood, a semi-rural
district whose houses with their private gardens attracted artists and
courtesans. Sarah confessed to being uncomfortable at such an address but it
was necessary. "I have had more trouble than you can imagine."

Willie had suffered a mental and physical breakdown following his
admission to the Bar in July 1858. Sarah explained Willie's illness as over
excitement caused by chemistry experiments involving various gases, law
reading and travel preparations to join Amelia. Doctors consulted in July
indicated that Willie's problem was his nervous system and that he needed
to be kept quiet. As his condition worsened, the doctor prescribed
laudanum, an opiate. When Willie became over-excited, the attendant
mistreated him.

Wentworth refused to accept the doctor's recommendation that Willie be
committed to an institution and sought a second opinion. Another doctor
recommended country air and so the family had moved out from central
London. Sarah probably chose St Johns Wood because her half-brother's

widow, Sarah, and her family lived there at 26 William Street. Sarah Cox helped Sarah Wentworth to nurse Willie. Doctors visited him daily and his physical health seemed to improve after September but his mind remained ill. Sarah had little sympathy for Robert Hunt, who became anxious when he realised that his daughter's marriage arrangements were in jeopardy, considering that Hunt was not worthy of such a son-in-law. William Charles Wentworth, junior, died at St Johns Wood on 31 March 1859, aged 32.[28] Sarah grieved for her eldest son who had been "so like a child in being free from the evil that young men are tempted with...he had so many noble qualities...his nature...quite unfitted him for this world...here he had so much trouble".[29]

At the height of Willie's illness, Fitzwilliam sailed for New Zealand to take up a sheep station. His parents accepted that his health could not survive the English climate. He travelled out with his aunt and uncle, Eliza and D'Arcy Wentworth, in December 1858. "A very spirited and determined fellow," he wanted to brave Thomas Fisher to see Timmie before he left.[30]

Wentworth had himself planned to return to the colony a few months later, in April 1859, leaving Sarah and Willie behind if Willie was not well enough to travel. Legal troubles rather than his son's illness changed these plans. In February 1859 he met T.S. Mort and discovered that his former partner, J. Lloyd, now owned his station on the Namoi. Believing that he had been the victim of a conspiracy to defraud him, on 24 March 1859 Wentworth filed proceedings against J.C. Lloyd, T.S. Mort, John Croft, Robert Tooth, William Mort, E.H. Lloyd and C.W. Lloyd.[31]

While her husband went to Rome for another sitting for his statue, Sarah busied herself buying furniture to redecorate Vaucluse. She went to Worcester for china, to Paris for wallpapers, then with her husband to Germany to purchase furniture for the best rooms. Twenty-five cases of furniture, weighing almost 40 tonnes, were despatched from Hamburg in November 1859. Travel and shopping sprees did not take Sarah's mind off Willie's death. Even the thought of her beloved Vaucluse did not cheer her because Willie, who had loved it so much, would never inherit it.[32]

November 1859 found Sarah back in London looking for a house to rent for three months, hoping the legal matters would be resolved by February 1860 so that they could leave for New South Wales. A house near a riding school would be ideal, for Didy, now 21 and the eldest of her unmarried daughters, would then be able to continue her riding lessons. They leased The Ferns at 6 Grove End, St Johns Wood in December. Torn between the educational and social opportunities for the children in Britain and their desire to return to Australia, William and Sarah dithered. Perhaps Sarah should remain in England with the children while Wentworth went back

 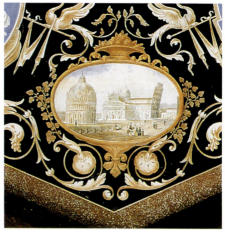

A souvenir of Sarah Wentworth's visits to Italy in the late 1850s.
Handpainted marble table-top decorated with Italian scenes
(detail showing Campanile, Pisa) *Vaucluse House Collection.*

alone. Perhaps D'Arcy, now 12, should be left in England at Harrow or Eton and the others return to the colony. Sarah could not bear this option: "dear Willie I consented to part with thinking it was for his own good — we know what suffering he had." When they learnt that D'Arcy would not be accepted at Harrow until he was 14, they decided to take the whole family to New South Wales as soon as Wentworth had given evidence in the first stage of the Lloyd case and return in two years to complete the legal proceedings when D'Arcy was old enough to go to Harrow. Sarah mused: "I must be content to give up dear old Vaucluse if Papa and the rest prefer returning." In the interim D'Arcy was sent to Mr Selwyn's school at Blackheath, a village well-known in the 1850s for its good schools.[33]

Fanny's confinement with her third child, due in August 1860, further delayed their departure as they would not travel the overland Red Sea route in summer. Restlessly they wandered from hotel to hotel, filling in the months till they could leave. They went to Hamburg to take the waters, to Yorkshire to see the Fitzwilliam Wentworth family tomb and to Brighton for Christmas because London was dreary. The girls continued their music and language lessons, Italian and German, in hotel sitting rooms. Sarah was delighted that Didy, Laura and Edith were often called the three graces and admired "for their amiable and ladylike qualities." Yet the girls were rarely in good health. Didy, the beauty of the family, fell from her horse in late 1860

Eliza Sophia [Didy] Wentworth (1838-1898).
Portrait in pastel by Adelaide Ironside, 1860. *Private Collection.*

Laura Wentworth (1842-1887).
Portrait in pastel by Adelaide Ironside, 1860. *Private Collection.*

and lay unconscious for an hour. A deep cut above her eyebrow left her in delicate health, suffering recurrent headaches that made her dependent on heavy medication for the rest of her life. Eighteen-year old Laura was under the care of a spine specialist for most of 1860 and Edith had also been ill. With her husband now approaching his seventies, death was increasingly in Sarah's thoughts. She worried that he might die before their affairs could be settled. "If we are spared" frequently qualified her plans.[34]

Back in London in the new year, their departure date finally set for 20 February 1861, they took a house in Harley Street, Cavendish Square for a few weeks while Sarah frantically packed, shopped and engaged servants to take with them. Wentworth presided over a colonial dinner at the Clarendon Hotel. One guest commented that Wentworth would be more at home in the colony dealing with the "mobocracy" than attending ceremonial affairs for which "God and Nature little fitted him."[35] William and Sarah with their four youngest children — Didy, Laura, Edith and D'Arcy — finally sailed for New South Wales on the *Benares*, arriving in Sydney in April 1861.

CHAPTER 6

Interlude: Mistress of Vaucluse

IN THE EIGHT YEARS since Sarah had lived in New South Wales, much had changed. Gold discoveries continued to bring wealth and a diverse population. Self-government, the object of her husband's lifetime in politics, had been achieved. A two house system of parliament had operated since 1856 and the right to vote had been extended to most male residents in 1858. By coincidence, the Wentworths returned to a colony in the midst of political and constitutional turmoil.

Wentworth's name still aroused strong feelings. There had been a violent debate in 1857 over whether his portrait should hang in the Legislative Assembly, and the news that he was returning to Sydney provoked further arguments about his contribution to the colony. After lengthy discussions, a public holiday was declared for the day of his return. As the *Benares* steamed along the coast toward Sydney on 18 April 1861, Richard Hill sailed out from Coogee with a copy of the address of welcome that was to be presented to Wentworth so that he could write a reply. A flotilla of boats carrying a crowd estimated at 900 to 1,000 met the *Benares* at the entrance to Sydney Harbour. As the procession of boats headed to Sydney Cove, the *Benares* slowed as it drew abreast of Vaucluse Bay. There was no role for Sarah and the children in the public reception that awaited the elder statesman and they were put ashore at Vaucluse. At Circular Quay, as the one o'clock gun was fired from Fort Macquarie, a crowd of politicians and gentry, townsfolk and a few Aborigines greeted Wentworth. After the speeches, Hill took him by carriage to Vaucluse.[1]

Sarah was happy to be home.

> Vaucluse is such a charming place that after seeing other Countries I think it more beautiful.... if I am spared many years I would return to this place to end my days and I wish to have a spot consecrated so that we may all rest together in our native place and I hope Papa may be allowed to leave(?) his remains here whenever and wherever he may be for his country has in his life proved(?) worthy(?) of him.[2]

Her sister, Maria Hunt, had lived at Vaucluse since the tenant left in 1858 but Sarah found her home almost uninhabitable from years of neglect.

Before the new French wallpapers and furniture could be shown to advantage, extensive repairs and renovations were essential. J.F. Hilly, architect, was engaged and stonemasons, carpenters and ironfounders employed. Modern facilities, such as water closets and dressing rooms, the comforts to which they had become accustomed in their cosmopolitan existence, were added by attaching a timber wing to the rear of the bedroom wing. Expense was no object, Wentworth informing Timmie that the considerable outlay on the house and grounds was trifling. Sarah enthusiastically replanted the gardens and orchards, adding several varieties of melons because her husband was fond of them. She was particularly happy gardening, purchasing sets of small garden tools for her own and her daughters' use. Drains and fences, too, came under her careful, practical attention. She checked levels in the cellar, purchased pumps, lead piping and cross-cut saws and directed the storage of the garden roller for the lawn and old timbers from a demolished shed that might one day be useful. On the bay in front of the house, she ordered a section of the beach enclosed with tea-tree fencing so that they could swim without fear of sharks.[3]

In June 1861 Wentworth accepted the presidency of the Legislative Council. The initial five-year appointments of members of the council had expired the previous month amid controversy. Robertson's land laws were due to come before the council but, anticipating that the upper house would reject the legislation, the government attempted to swamp the council by nominating new members who would support the legislation. On 10 May 1861 the president of the Legislative Council, Sir William Burton, resigned in protest, as did most councillors. Without a quorum, the legislation could not proceed and the terms of office of the councillors expired the following day. The next councillors would be appointed for life. Wentworth's appointment as president was acceptable in this crisis because of his standing as an elder statesman and because he would serve only a short term as he had to return to England to settle his legal affairs. He held office from 24 June 1861 to 9 October 1862. Sarah proudly sent Timmie a photograph of him in his robes at the opening of parliament in 1862.[4]

D'Arcy was enrolled at Sydney Grammar School from May 1861 to September 1862. The younger girls, Laura and Edith, took music and singing lessons with Mrs Logan, who since the early 1840s had taught the daughters of the colonial élite. Seventeen-year-old Edith also read history with Miss Sharpe, her governess, and with Laura spent the rest of the day playing with her dogs and gardening. Didy, in her mid-twenties, helped her mother with "a little housekeeping". Social introductions for Didy, Laura and Edith proved less traumatic than their older sisters' experiences.[5]

Her husband's unexpected return to public life meant that once again

Vaucluse in 1869. The iron verandah was added when the family returned to the colony 1861-1862. Pencil sketch by Rebecca Martens. *Dixson Library.*

Sarah faced Sydney's social élite. Years of travel abroad had given her confidence and a wider circle of acquaintances. Several of the leading families had enjoyed Wentworth's hospitality in London or Paris, where Sarah had regularly entertained colonial expatriates. The new governor, Sir John Young, with Lady Young had arrived in Sydney only the month before Wentworth returned. Sarah had already met them on Corfu, where Young had been administrator when Joody died, and again in London at a reception to congratulate Young on his appointment as governor of New South Wales. Wentworth soon became a favourite with Lady Young. The period of mourning following the death of Wentworth's brother, 67-year-old D'Arcy, in

79

July 1861 provided a time for quiet testing of colonial attitudes to Sarah and her family, who were now joined by D'Arcy's widow, Eliza, who came to live at Vaucluse.

Lady Young changed the social calendar, postponing the season for parties and balls until summer had passed. In the pre-season interlude of late 1861, Sarah was relieved that she and her family were accepted. Writing to Timmie in September 1861, Sarah boasted that "all the nice families...call on us". By the time the social season opened in early 1862, the Wentworth girls, too, were favourites with Lady Young and invited to her parties at Government House. Invitations followed for Sarah and the girls to attend the Queen's Birthday Ball, charity functions, like the ball for the School of Industry, and private dinners at the homes of leading citizens, all occasions from which Sarah had once been excluded. Sarah's pleasure in these invitations was not diminished by her awareness that "Papa of course is the reason". She felt that, on the surface at least, Sydney had changed. "There are no exclusive settlers to all appearances and therefore you do not hear of...envy and malice".[6]

Fitz came across from New Zealand in mid-1861 for a brief visit to see his parents, and to borrow money from his father.[7] Sarah's favourite niece, Mary Doyle, brought her children to visit Vaucluse for Christmas 1861 and stayed for six months. Sarah was impressed by Mary's efforts to raise her children, despite a drunken husband. She gave her clothes and persuaded Wentworth to give Mary an annuity of £50 and some cows when she returned to Maitland. Mary's children were not the only ones to benefit from Sarah's interest and affection. Perhaps missing her grandchildren in England, she took an interest in the welfare of the other children at Vaucluse, the families of the servants who lived on the estate. Some of the servants had been with the family for many years, a few living in huts on Vaucluse when they became too old to work. The death of her old coachman in April 1862 depressed Sarah, reminding her of a happier past when her family were all around her.[8]

Tenerani's statue of Wentworth arrived in November 1861. Sarah was pleased with the likeness and the beauty of the workmanship. After some debate about where it should be placed, the Senate of the University of Sydney grudgingly agreed to put the statue in the new Great Hall. It was unveiled by the governor on 23 June 1862 to an audience composed mainly of ladies, robed university dignitaries, foreign consuls and the military. James Martin delivered a eulogy on Wentworth's achievements. It was not an occasion, though, of personal triumph. Political commentary was banned by the Senate, as was Wentworth himself, "it having been decided I ought not to be there". The balance of public funds that had been raised for the statue

Sir John Young, Governor of New South Wales 1861-1867,
and Lady Young. *Mitchell Library.*

was given to the university for a travelling scholarship.[9]

On the evening of Wednesday 17 September 1862, William and Sarah Wentworth gave a ball. This was the only occasion on which they entertained publicly in New South Wales. Sarah started preparations for her ball in June, moving the venue from the new verandahs of Vaucluse to a rented mansion when Roslyn Hall became available in mid-July. In the midst of the gentry enclave of Woolloomooloo Hill, Roslyn Hall was "more like a palace than a private house". Built in 1834 for the engineer and miller Thomas Barker, it was offered for auction on 14 July 1862. The enormous stone mansion, elegantly decorated with gilded frescoes in the drawing room, was more conveniently situated than distant Vaucluse. Sarah was delighted when she obtained the services of a good cook who, having worked at Government House, brought extra prestige to the entertainment. George Hill, her sister's brother-in-law, a jovial butcher and former mayor of Sydney, assisted Sarah with the preparations. Her guests included the governor and his wife, members of the Legislative Council, government ministers and

81

many of the "first people", the ultimate social triumph for the "damned whore".[10]

Sarah had no leisure to revel in her social coup. The following day she started to pack up Vaucluse ready for their return to England. Wentworth decided against leasing Vaucluse and invited Maria Hunt and her husband to stay as caretakers until they returned. Depressed at having to leave Vaucluse just as she had put everything in order, Sarah hoped they would return soon as "this climate is better for Old People—if Papa and I are spared we hope to end our days here". Even the girls confessed that they were sorry to leave Vaucluse. William and Sarah Wentworth, with Didy, Laura, Edith, D'Arcy and widowed sister-in-law Eliza Wentworth, sailed on the *Bombay* on 22 October 1862, bound for England via Melbourne, Ceylon, Port Suez and overland to Alexandria.[11]

On their departure Governor Sir John Young wrote to the Colonial Office, praising Wentworth as "the colonist most distinguished by genius and services" and recommending him for a knighthood. This praise was formally noted by the Colonial Office but no honours were conferred, though it was rumoured that Wentworth had declined to accept a knighthood.[12]

CHAPTER 7

Expatriate

THEY RETURNED TO Europe with no fixed intentions, beyond educating D'Arcy and resolving Wentworth's legal battles. Loss of their heavy luggage and papers, which were following on another vessel that was wrecked, added to the difficulties of managing property half a world away. Winter 1862 and most of 1863 found them commuting between London and Paris. In early 1864 they were in elegant, lively Brighton, Wentworth's preferred resort when he was bored. Judgement in *Wentworth* v. *Lloyd* had been handed down in April 1863 against Wentworth, who immediately launched an appeal, disregarding the costs which would probably amount to the value of the property in dispute. The appeal judgement, upholding the original decision, was announced in May 1864. Wentworth was devastated. Now as "deaf as a post," he suddenly looked ten years older.[1]

More than a year had passed since they had sailed from Sydney yet they still had no fixed address. Wentworth wanted to rent a house on the outskirts of London with gardens for the girls and hothouses to amuse himself but it was difficult to find a large house in a good situation for less than £600 per year. Sarah would have preferred furnishing her own home but, although her husband's income was considerable, he could not spare the money and so they searched for a furnished house. Finally, in October 1864, they rented 5 Lancaster Gate for £650 per year. A well-furnished and roomy house, it had three floors of bedrooms, dining and drawing room floors, servants' quarters and a basement kitchen. This was their home for the next three years.

In the summer of 1867 they moved to the country and rented Coombe Lodge overlooking the River Thames at Pangbourne, near Reading. A mansion in the classical style, built about 1784 for a wealthy East India merchant, its grounds had been landscaped by the fashionable gardener Humphrey Repton. The winters at Coombe, however, were too cold for Sarah and the girls, the house and grounds were expensive to maintain and restricted their freedom to wander to Paris or Nice or dream of returning to Sydney and so their restless search for a comfortable home began again. In November 1869 they leased Merly House, outside Bournemouth in Dorset, for £450 a year. The three storey house, built about 1760 and still famous for the grand

Coombe Lodge, Pangbourne, residence of the Wentworth
family 1867-1869. *Vaucluse House Collection.*

library wing that had been demolished in the 1820s, looked across the Stour
Valley and the town of Wimborne. Set in six acres of gardens, it was
approached by a serpentine drive through the woods. Sarah was pleased that
there were fewer grass lawns to maintain. The adjoining 2,000 acres (800
hectares) could be leased out for shooting and fishing, returning about £200.
The private apartments included 18 bedrooms, with bathroom and dressing
room, but it was the public rooms that attracted comment, especially the
lofty reception room with its florid, rococo decoration, statues, pictures and
organ. Although Merly was only a mile from Wimborne station and trains
to London, Wentworth, despite his age and ill-health, soon became restless.

Within two years, he wanted to live closer to the metropolis.[2]

In England, as at Vaucluse, Sarah's responsibility was to manage the household. Their wealth meant that she lived as a lady, required to do little physical work herself. She hired and paid the servants and supervised their work in the house and grounds. Female servants changed regularly because the family moved so often. Her household staff in London included a cook, a kitchen maid and a lady's maid who was also a good needlewoman. In the country they employed more servants to maintain the grounds. Male servants, particularly Wentworth's personal attendants, changed less frequently. Old William Miles and the younger James had cared for the now elderly Wentworth for more than a decade. One servant aroused more comment than the others. Bobby, an Aborigine from Vaucluse, came to Europe with them in 1862, but after three cold English winters, he wanted to go home. He was a curiosity for their European acquaintances, to whom he was introduced as a "chief in his own country."[3]

> We will all be sorry when he goes but it is a pity that we ever brought him away from Mrs Hunt who would always have taken good care of him. He is naturally so clever and sensible that I hope he will be content to go back to Vaucluse.[4]

William approached the government and Sarah considered seeking the support of a well-known preacher to assist Bobby and his people. Eventually they arranged for Bobby to return to Vaucluse in the care of their neighbour, Sir Daniel Cooper of Woollahra. Sarah sympathised with Bobby's homesickness. Transplanted gum trees did not thrive like oaks. "You will not be surprised at my dislike for this Country...it is not the place for us Australians."[5]

"Papa is dull if he remains in one place long — I am fond of flower and outdoor work so that I do not require the same change",[6] wrote Sarah to her son-in-law. She spent much of her time in the gardens of Coombe and Merly, sending seeds back to Vaucluse more as an act of faith that she would return than with any real expectation that its grounds would be developed in her absence. Their rented homes were large for a family of five adults, but spare bedrooms were always ready for house guests. Sarah was a gregarious person and liked to have people around her. Her hospitality continued the pattern established in the colony, a preference for house guests rather than more formal or lavish entertainments. A constant procession of grandchildren, relatives and friends, casual acquaintances and visiting colonists stayed, sometimes for days, often for months. Their acquaintances, met in fashionable health resorts in southern England and Europe, were often retired military and colonial officials. Others were

A fashionable gathering at The Pavilion, Brighton, a resort
favoured by the Wentworth family. *Illustrated London News*, 1867.

impoverished colonists, like Adelaide and Martha Ironside whom Sarah
befriended.[7]

The household revolved around Wentworth's health and moods. Sarah,
assisted by Laura, nursed him in ill-health and sought diversions for him
when he was well. Traditional and homeopathic remedies were tried to
relieve his pains and they travelled to take mineral baths at well-known
resorts. "Papa is well", wrote Laura to her sister, "but when he feels pretty
well he begins again to be careless about himself". His daughters blamed his
troubles on too much wine, which he denied, but Sarah agreed that he was
not prudent. He was easily tired by exertion and heart disease was diagnosed
in 1869. From 1870 he was confined to a chair. Deafness added to the
difficulty of entertaining him. Now in her sixties, Sarah's health was usually

'The Three Graces', Edith, Eliza and Laura, daughters of Sarah and
William Charles Wentworth. Group portrait in oils by H.J. Gruder, 1868.
Vaucluse House Collection.

robust, except for trouble reading in dim evening light and she resolved this
by investing in a large-print Bible for herself and her husband.[8]

> Papa takes up so much of my time now that he is not able to walk about — he
> looks well in the face but he is very feeble…and poor man he is so patient for
> he sits in his Easey chair day after day and about 7 o'clock he is quite ready to
> go to bed he is carried up stairs in a chair we bought him.[9]

When his health permitted, travel provided a diversion. They went to
Ireland, not only to see Dublin, the Killarney Lakes and Blarney Castle, but
to seek out Wentworth relations at Portadown, Dundalk and Armagh. Their
travels did not include a return to the homes of Sarah's antecedents in
Broseley or Norwich. Visits to fashionable spa resorts and seaside towns
combined the pleasures of a holiday with health cures.[10] Sarah and the girls

were reluctant to let Wentworth go anywhere alone, though he escaped their vigilance to visit a coal mine, near Cardiff, in which he had shares, or to stay at his club in London to conduct business and maintain contact with a network of colonial expatriates in London. Part of the circle around Sir Charles Nicholson, Wentworth was too infirm to play an active role in their social or political affairs, beyond attending colonial dinners to support projects such as the foundation of the Royal Commonwealth Society and entertaining them at family dinners when he and Sarah were in London.[11] Outspoken and direct in manner, many still found him an unlikeable man and his daughters' friends were variously terrified, offended or bemused on meeting him.[12]

Ill-health and their restless wanderings gave the Wentworth girls few opportunities to have a regular social life. Nevertheless they had a wide circle of acquaintances drawn from family connections through Eliza Wentworth's family, the Macphersons, or Timmie and Fanny's evangelical friends the Fairfields, school friends and people met on foreign travels such as their singing teachers, the Marra family from Italy. When their father was well, or their brothers at home, they were escorted to parties, fancy dress balls, the opera and circus. With their auburn and golden hair, fashionably gowned, Didy, Laura and Edith were a distinctive trio.[13]

Wealthy enough to indulge in pleasure, they sought like many women in similar circumstances a sense of purpose and fulfilment through religion. Their guide in such matters was Timmie Fisher whose "whole Soul is bent on doing good and all for the Lord Jesus whom she loves as her life and actions plainly prove".[14]

Timmie's moral influence on the family was very strong because of, rather than despite, her enforced alienation. Fanny and Laura especially were drawn to personal evangelism, though not to involvement in public charitable institutions. Idle amusement increasingly frustrated Laura who, until they moved to Coombe Lodge, had no outlet for her philanthropic ambitions except nursing her father. In the village of Pangbourne she taught Sunday school and daily visited the poor in their cottages to read and pray with them. In general, Sarah did not object to Laura going alone to the village but she insisted that Laura be chaperoned by another evangelist, Miss Sykes, during her charity visits.[15]

Wentworth was the principal object of their missionary endeavours. Timmie, Fanny and especially Laura felt "very very sad to see Papa growing old without having found any real happiness in this world and without any hope or without any *just hope* for the next."[16] Timmie and Fanny sent their parents religious tracts which Laura read to her father and she nailed Biblical texts to the walls of his dressing room. Wentworth accepted his daughters'

Edith Wentworth (1845-1891).
Private Collection.

efforts with good humour. "If my Faith in Christianity is not so fervent as your own, do not therefore imagine that I am altogether an unbeliever. I have done and still do all I can to reconcile my Doubts and I hope ultimately to remove them."[17]

Sarah did not entirely share the evangelical enthusiasms of her daughters but she accompanied them to hear the latest popular preacher, read the books Timmie and Fanny sent her, sewed and dressed dolls for church bazaars. "I frankly confess that I do not love my Jesus as I know I ought, but I never forget to ask Him to guide me and to forgive me".[18] Worried that Laura's passion to evangelise the poor was "too much of a good thing" and would ruin her health, Sarah intervened and refused to allow her to undergo adult baptism. Didy and Edith, too, were sceptical. To please Timmie, Edith learnt two verses and read a chapter of the Bible every day "but I don't see that it will do me any good — for though I have a sort of half belief that what you have said is all true I can't realise or feel it myself". Years later, Didy and Fanny joined the Swedenborg New Church, to Edith's dismay as she then found less pleasure in their company.[19]

D'Arcy had been sent to a school in Fulham. In August 1864, at the age of 16, he entered the Royal Military College at Sandhurst and, after a year's training, passed his examinations. He wanted to join a cavalry regiment, preferably the 7th Hussars, but had to settle for a cornet's commission purchased in the 8th King's Royal Irish Hussars. Stationed at Aldershot from July 1865, his regiment moved to Scotland in 1868, when D'Arcy was promoted to lieutenant. A careless, indulged young man with expensive tastes, his extravagances worried his parents and Sarah still would not leave him alone in England. He resigned his commission in early 1870, claiming that the idle life of a cavalry officer encouraged him to spend too much. Wentworth allowed D'Arcy £500 in addition to his military pay but this was not enough for his horses, dress, wine and servants.[20]

Sarah was also concerned about the relationship between her husband and Fitzwilliam. Wentworth had arranged in 1860 a £10,000 mortgage for Fitz, secured on the property Fitz would inherit from his grandfather's will, thereby avoiding encumbering Wentworth's personal estates so late in his life. By 1861, when a formal deed of partnership was drafted, Wentworth had also advanced Fitz at least £21,000 for his stations in New Zealand. Fitz was appointed manager, with no salary, and was forbidden to speculate or sell the stations without his father's approval. Despite this agreement, Fitz paid his cousin Henry Hill to manage the stations. He then sold out for almost £63,000, without consulting his father, and travelled to America with James Hill in the mid-1860s. Fitz preferred colonial life and took little pleasure in his regular trips to England on family business.[21]

Sarah worried, too, about the increasing influence of the Hill family on Fitzwilliam. "My dear Fitz will be like his Father easily inspired it would be a pity if any one had much influence on him when we are gone."[22] Her concern deepened when Fitz announced his engagement to Mary Jane Hill, second daughter of George Hill:

> we must make up our minds for his sake to treat his wife as we ought for then she will be one of our family — the poor fellow will have his regrets for he knows that he has not chosen as his Father would wish — not as regards the girl for I believe she is very amiable[23]

She thought Timmie should not attend the wedding but her husband was more philosophic, instructing Timmie not to interfere or offend Fitz. Fitzwilliam and Mary were married at St Michael's, Surry Hills in March 1868 and left almost immediately for his new station near Dunedin, New Zealand, his father having lent him £24,000 a few months earlier to purchase a station. Any doubts Sarah had about her daughter-in-law were overcome when she finally met Mary in 1871.[24]

Thomas Fisher persisted in refusing to acknowledge the Wentworth family. The absurd situation now angered Sarah. If

> Mr Fisher thinks your family a disgrace to him he is the only one that think so — and the paper that was sent to you ought to make you proud of a Father that so many of his fellow creatures respect and you ought to repel with scorn any remark made against your parents.[25]

Eliza Wentworth's presence continued to provide the aura of respectability required before Fisher would permit his wife to visit her family. The younger Wentworth girls did not know Fisher by sight and often wondered if they had passed him in a crowd. From the Wentworths' return to England in 1862, Sarah was allowed to see her Fisher grandchildren and she was delighted when Alice, Willie, Robert and Donny Fisher were allowed to stay with her. Nonetheless, Sarah and the girls remained excessively careful about meeting Timmie and avoiding contact with Fisher.[26]

Fisher had been in financial difficulties and poor health from 1862. When his daughter, Alice, became seriously ill in February 1866, Wentworth wrote offering assistance. Sarah and the girls were willing to help in nursing Alice. Fisher curtly replied that as he had not corresponded with Wentworth since 1854, he saw no need to do so now and any help from Wentworth was "altogether out of the question". Fisher's problems reached a crisis a few months later and this time he accepted his father-in-law's intervention. Wentworth lent Fisher at least £5,000.

It was an opportunity that William and Sarah accepted without hesitation. Admitting no favourites among their children, nevertheless, their

Fitzwilliam Wentworth (1833-1915) and his wife
Mary Jane (nee Hill) (c.1840-1924). *Vaucluse House Collection.*

first-born Timmie had a special place in their affections, particularly her
father's, which the years of alienation had only intensified. With no allusion
to past injustices or his son-in-law's abilities, Wentworth proposed that
Fisher return to New South Wales, re-establish his legal business and manage
Wentworth's affairs. Vaucluse was not let, though Sarah's sister Maria Hunt
and her family were living there. Preferring that his daughter, rather than his
sister-in-law, be mistress of Vaucluse he offered the Fishers Vaucluse, rent
free. Nor did Fisher need to repay the money as it would have been
Timmie's when her father died.[27]

Recognising the trust that had been unquestioningly placed in him by his
parents-in-law, Fisher finally apologised for having estranged himself from the
family for so many years. The Fishers returned to the colony on the *Jason* in
late 1866. By coincidence, among the passengers were John Cox's widow and
daughter, also seeking a new life in the colony. During the voyage, Timmie
learnt about her grandfather, convict Francis Cox, an aspect of the family
that Sarah had chosen not to tell her children. Though Willie had learnt

Entrance Hall, Vaucluse in 1869 when occupied by Thomasine Fisher and her family. Pencil sketch by Rebecca Martens. *Dixson Library.*

Sarah Wentworth's sisters and brothers-in-law: *(top)* Maria Hunt (nee Cox)
(1809-1885) and Robert Allen Hunt (c.1805-1892); *(bottom)* Henrietta Hill (nee Cox)
(1812-1892) and Richard Hill (1810-1895). *Private Collections.*

the truth in the late 1840s, the others were not told. Sarah urged Timmie and her husband to call at Government House when they had settled at Vaucluse. They need not go into society but they should establish their position and eligibility to move in colonial society.[28]

Timmie's aunts, Maria Hunt and Henrietta Hill, did not welcome her return or her husband's appointment as Wentworth's agent. Though the commission Wentworth paid his agent was only £300-400 per year, the potential influence was considerable, involving management not only of the Vaucluse, Homebush and Toongabbie estates but control of the rental and sale of city properties, land on the north shore and along the South Head roads, general supervision of pastoral properties and the income from wool clips and meat sales. Sarah's sisters and their husbands quarrelled with the Fishers, refusing to vacate Vaucluse and inciting tenants to withold rent payments. The vicious and petty campaigns that followed included threats to prosecute Timmie and her husband for slander, stripping unripened fruit from the orchards of Vaucluse and uprooting the banana plantation.[29]

Sarah was annoyed that her sister would not provide Timmie with an inventory of items at Vaucluse. "Mrs Hunt could have done so much better and if I had been in her place I would have done so."[30] One of the conditions of the Hunts living at Vaucluse had been that Mary Doyle and her children could always find refuge there and Sarah was appalled when she learnt that they had been turned away. Timmie worried that she had created a split between her mother and aunts but Sarah urged her not to be so "weak minded" and recognise that it was better for her mother to know their true nature.[31] The dispute with the Hunts and Hills was made more complex and stressful because Amelia Hunt was staying with Sarah and William in England during 1867-68 and Fitzwilliam had just become engaged to Mary Hill.[32]

Unpleasantness among the Wentworths, Fishers, Hunts, Hills and Todhunters took a more sinister turn with the tragic death of Willie Fisher in April 1868. Tales of immoral behaviour and suicide hinted yet again at something innately improper about Sarah and William Wentworth and their family.

Timmie had been having problems in England managing her 22-year-old son. Trained as an accountant, Willie Fisher wanted to learn about the pastoral industry. Initially he was to go to New Zealand, but when he convinced his grandmother that he was willing to accept the harsh conditions of outback life she arranged for him to work on Wentworth's station on Marthaguy Creek, west of the Castlereagh River, where Sarah's nephews Frank, James and William Todhunter also worked. Sarah thought that Willie would progress with the Todhunters to instruct him and watch over him.[33]

Wentworth had occupied runs on the Marthaguy since the 1830s. In the early 1850s he joined John Christie, formerly manager of one of his Riverina stations, in a partnership on the Cullemburrawang, Collyburl and Inglegar runs, later known as Haddon Riggs. Employing a few Europeans as managers and a large number of Aborigines as stockmen, by the 1860s Wentworth and Christie ran cattle and sheep over 16 runs covering 400 square miles (103,600 hectares) of myall and saltbush, fine grazing land with an 18 mile (29 kilometre) frontage along the Marthaguy Creek and four miles (6 kilometres) on the Macquarie River.

Willie Fisher arrived at Haddon Riggs in late 1866 and soon took one of the part-Aboriginal girls as his mistress. The station superintendent, S.C. Kirby, sent her away but she returned to Willie a few weeks later. When one of the Aboriginal men wanted to take her back to live with him, Willie Fisher refused and locked her in his hut. While Willie was away working, Kirby ordered the Aborigine to take the girl, her clothes and a horse and leave, but when Willie discovered that she had gone, he went after them with a gun. James Todhunter met him looking for the Aborigine, took Willie's gun and horse and told him to walk back to the head station. No-one worried when Willie did not return for several days, thinking that he had found the girl and gone bush with her. Three weeks later, on 6 May 1868, shepherds found Willie's body. A broken leather strap on a tree and the position of the remains indicated that Willie had hung himself.[34]

"I fear it will break Mama's heart", Laura wrote to Timmie when they learnt of Willie's death.

> Poor Mama reproaches herself so bitterly that she did not more often write to him. She was only prevented from writing by the thought that Mr Christie and the others might shew him less kindness if they saw him receiving much notice from her and that *trusting them* as she did with him they would love him and care for him.[35]

Distressed that, without Willie's protection, the Aboriginal girl might be mistreated by her people or the men on the station, the Wentworth girls urged Timmie to find and help her, confident that her well-being would have been Willie's last wish. They supported Timmie's idea to send a missionary to the Aborigines on the Marthaguy.[36]

Shocked, not by Willie's relationship with the Aboriginal girl, but at the thought that he would take his own life, Sarah was convinced that her grandson had been murdered. Her suspicion deepened with reports that Willie's life had been made miserable by Frank Todhunter who accused him of being old Wentworth's spy. Then came the disturbing news of the death in November 1868 of Wentworth's partner. John Christie had fallen down a bank in a fit of delirium tremens and drowned in the Macquarie River at Narromine. The

Sarah Wentworth in the 1860s.
Vaucluse House Collection.

Wentworths were accused of driving Christie to his death. Sarah emphatically rejected this. Aware of Christie's drinking problem, she had suggested Christie take a holiday as he had been outback too long. She believed that Christie's conscience troubled him when he learnt more about the circumstances of Willie's death, and that this led to depression, a drinking binge and his fatal accident.[37]

Neglected Haddon Riggs homestead with its uninhabited huts and woolshed and rumours of mysterious deaths provided ample material for speculation in the Dubbo and Sydney newspapers. Sarah felt that the Hunts and Hills had concealed from Timmie the circumstances at Haddon Riggs while Willie was alive. Wentworth was furious when he learnt that Richard Hill had sent Timmie a copy of Frank Todhunter's brutal account of Willie's last days. Sarah, too, suspected that the Todhunters were sending cruel letters to Timmie about Willie's death. In England Sarah received an insulting letter from Hunt making allegations about Willie Wentworth's relationship with his daughter. Threats were made to write to the *Times* giving details of the deaths of Willie Fisher and Christie and poison pen letters about the incident were sent to the colonel of D'Arcy's regiment. The vendetta continued with James Hill making life difficult for Robert Fisher at the bank where he worked in Sydney.[38]

The aura of tragedy remained for years. Christie and Wentworth's stations on the Macquarie River and the Marthaguy were put up for sale in early 1870. To his father's dismay, Fitz purchased Haddon Riggs head station and Frank Todhunter and George Hill purchased other portions. William G. Todhunter selected land on the Inglegar Run and the following year opened the Inglegar Hotel which he operated until his death in 1890. It was carried on by his widow, Maria Todhunter, nee Cox, daughter of Sarah's half-brother John Cox.[39]

Money was rarely a problem for Sarah, though she was a careful housekeeper. Wentworth was generous to his wife and daughters and, in addition, since her father's death in 1831 Sarah had received a small income from his property in Sydney. She regarded this income as her independence and had very strong ideas about her right to use the money as she chose. She was annoyed when her sister sent her rents from Cox's Wharf to Wentworth, "not that I object to his receiving it but I have the right to have it paid to whom I wish".[40]

With her husband housebound and sending contradictory instructions to his colonial agents, Sarah extended her involvement from the management of household affairs to the direction of all of Wentworth's business interests, making a deliberate effort to understand their complexities so that she need not worry him. Although she did not wish to intervene between Fitz and

William Charles Wentworth and daughter Laura who nursed him
for the last three years of his life. *Vaucluse House Collection.*

his father, Fitz was rarely in England to make the decisions. She
corresponded separately with Thomas Fisher and the station managers from
the mid-1860s and from the early 1870s kept a summary of stock numbers,
wool prices and receipts so that she could understand Fisher's letters to
Wentworth and convey them to her husband and son. Fisher was instructed
to make sure all their property deeds were registered as her husband had
always been very careless about such details. She was aware of the value of
the coal seams on their Newcastle property, of the export potential of the
coal and the value of the timber, and she understood the importance of
good management for such resources.

Taking responsibility for the sale of stock, she followed Wentworth's
general instructions about the sale of their stations, disappointed that he
wanted to dispose of them because of the drought of the late 1860s. Sarah
was more optimistic, believing that the men (Wentworth, Fitz and Fisher)
were too easily dismayed by drought and low prices, too hasty in selling and

too afraid of the future. She had lived through depression before; she knew the fear and knew also that better seasons would come. Her enthusiasm for the future extended to projects for meat preserving and refrigeration, about which she was informed by Augustus Morris, a friend of the family since the 1840s, who was experimenting with meat exports. Willie Fisher's tragic example kept her alive to the dangers of station management. When Robert Fisher indicated that he wanted to manage a property, she told his father that they should look first for a sensible wife for Robert, a woman who would "keep him from becoming a bushman of the inferior class for when there is no formal society they often get into poor Mr Christie's state."[41]

D'Arcy's decision in 1870 to leave the army opened the possibility for their return to the colony. Sarah considered schemes for D'Arcy and his sisters to live in New Zealand with Fitz but it was already too late for Wentworth.

> I do not agree…that returning to the Colony will…prolong my life but whether or not I do not think I shall undertake the voyage unless in some urgent necessity which I do not consider exists at present….It is true that Mrs W has a longing to see the colony and she may perhaps go out there some of these days…but I doubt…whether she will get me to accompany her. I am getting very ricketty and infirm and I should dread the voyage…; but she is comparatively active and will be able to bear it.[42]

He wanted Vaucluse to be put in order but not improved so that Sarah would have a home "endeared to her…by so many recollections". He did not expect to see it, or Timmie, again. This reality did not stop Sarah planning frantically to take him back to Vaucluse.[43]

Fitzwilliam brought his wife to England in 1871. They were shipwrecked at the Cape *en route* and their baby daughter died on the voyage. He found his father "unequal to any lengthened mental exercise or capable of long fixing his thoughts…and his memory…very weak and uncertain". Both Didy and Laura looked ill from their hermit-like existence nursing their father but Sarah looked "wonderfully young and beyond being a little stouter not a day altered" from when Fitz had seen her five years before. Neither his mother nor sisters had any firm ideas about what they would do when Wentworth died.

> They talk in the same breath of a House in London, of a place in the country, of going abroad, or to Australia and it is quite evident that the wandering and desultory life they have led for the last twenty years has quite unsettled them.[44]

With their lease at Merly House due to expire in June 1872, Fitz worried about their future. He, too, doubted his father could survive the voyage back to Vaucluse. Recognising that the end could not be long, he left his wife and newborn son, another William Charles Wentworth, born at Merly in September

Merly House, Wimborne, Dorset, residence of the Wentworth
family 1869-1872. *Private Collection.*

1871, to hurry back to New Zealand and settle his affairs so that he could
remain in England until his father died.[45]

William Charles Wentworth died at Merly on 20 March 1872. Sarah
grieved for her loss.

> it is still like a dream to me I can not realise it though I see the empty chair
> and the light of our dwelling has left us so desolate for he was the one that
> made our house so very cheerful.... When I looked on him so peacefully passing
> from this world I could not help thinking how grand and noble he seemed even
> in his weakness and even at that — the saddest trial of my life I looked on him
> with admiration of God's noblest work for I knew every turn(?) of his character,
> even his weakness I could not blame — only pity was the true reply my heart
> could give to him who was so very truthful that he was so often deceived like a
> child... how truly his country have judged him it was the first love of his heart
> when he was young and the last inspiration.[46]

101

Sarah Wentworth's instructions to her son-in-law,
Thomas Fisher, to prepare the family mausoleum, 1872.
Wentworth Papers. Mitchell Library.

CHAPTER 8

Widow

WENTWORTH'S DEATH, though long awaited, left Sarah and her daughters without a sense of purpose. For so many years, their lives had revolved around caring for him. Now, free to order their own affairs, they were undecided what to do. Fitzwilliam learnt of his father's death on his way back to England. Arriving a few weeks later, he found his mother and sisters "all looking very much worn and distressed". He despaired of making arrangements for them. "They are all so utterly impracticable and so greatly averse to living in Sydney that I can hardly conjecture yet what they will ultimately do."[1] Sarah was ambivalent about living at Vaucluse, uncertain if the memories of happier days would be a comfort or a trial, wondering how she would adjust to what had once been a household dominated by one man and ten laughing children: "It requires a number of persons to make Vaucluse cheerful I think I should be very melancoley if I were there with few people around me".[2]

Laura and Edith went to Brussels for a holiday while Fitzwilliam, Sarah and Didy managed the legal details and arrangements to bury Wentworth in Australia. Wentworth had left personal property valued at under £60,000, investments of £54,000 and various bank shares. Reeve, Fisher and James Milson all declined to act as executors, leaving the burden of the complicated trust arrangements to Fitzwilliam and Sarah.[3] Sarah and the girls would have liked to erect in St Andrew's Cathedral a marble tomb with recumbent figure, just like the one their Wentworth ancestors had in York Minster, but they suspected that people in Sydney would object to such a memorial and so abandoned the idea. Wentworth had wanted to be buried inside a large rock at Vaucluse, near Parsley Bay. Fisher was instructed to measure and photograph the site so that the rock could be hewn out and enough shelves cut for the coffins, not only of Wentworth, but of other family members, so that they would all rest together. Sarah went to Brussels to select a marble door, interior fittings and landscape designs for the mausoleum surroundings.[4]

As arrangements to bring Wentworth's body back to Vaucluse progressed, it became likely that only Sarah, Didy and Fitz would return to Australia. D'Arcy's marriage had been planned before his father died. Sarah was happy about it, believing that if D'Arcy had the inclination to take a wife then he should do so. Perhaps then he would settle down. Fitzwilliam disagreed. D'Arcy was too extravagant and irresponsible to marry and his intended bride, Lucy Bowman, was much older than him. At Sarah's insistence and against his better judgement, Fitz lent her £2,000 so she could clear most of D'Arcy's debts, drawing as well on her and Didy's allowances to reduce the debts to £1,500. To repay the loan, Sarah would sell her half share in Cox's Wharf. D'Arcy had inherited the properties at Frederick's Valley and Orange. When large deposits of gold and copper were uncovered there in mid-1872, Sarah was relieved that D'Arcy had gained another substantial income because money went such a short way with him.[5]

Lucy Bowman probably met D'Arcy through her family's friendship with Fanny Reeve. Twice she broke off her engagement to D'Arcy, disturbed by his attitudes and uncertain that she really loved him. Finally she agreed to the marriage, hoping she would come to love him later. D'Arcy's marriage to Lucy Bowman took place at Bickley, south of London, on 15 October 1872 but was never consummated. On their European honeymoon, D'Arcy told her his feelings had changed, that he regarded her as a sister rather than a wife and suggested that she return to her mother. At Merly after their honeymoon, D'Arcy ordered the servants to put him in his old room and find another for Lucy. They would live independently, he said, she in Australia and he shooting in Africa for a year or two. When his indifference turned to anger and he raged that he had "not been *brute* enough to you", she fled terrified to her family. They provided no refuge, blaming her for the marriage breakdown.

Sarah, too, blamed Lucy, accusing her of marrying D'Arcy fully intending to refuse to fulfil her duty as his wife. Yet Sarah's over-protection of D'Arcy was probably as much to blame.

> Mrs Wentworth...where D'Arcy is concerned will not *listen* to reason....she has...done her utmost to ruin him from his childhood, but she may now see some of the fruits of it, in all this misery that has come upon two people.

Lucy Wentworth went to her older half-sister in Switzerland while her mother and sister sailed to New York to avoid the scandal. Lucy returned in the mid-1870s to London, where Sarah sought her out. D'Arcy paid Lucy a regular allowance but there was no reconciliation and they led separate lives until their deaths in the 1920s. Always in debt to his bookies, roving between England and Australia, in the mid-1880s D'Arcy formed a relationship with an Irish girl, Anne Reilly, by whom he had twin daughters, born in 1885. Responsibility was finally forced on him when Anne died in 1890, leaving him to raise the girls.[6]

D'Arcy Bland Wentworth (1848-1922) and Lucy Anne Bowman in
the 1860s; they married in 1872. *Private Collections.*

D'Arcy was not alone in making an impetuous and unhappy marriage in
1872. His sisters became rich women on Wentworth's death, each inheriting
on her thirtieth birthday or upon marriage £25,000 or an annual allowance
of about £2,000, at a time when few men earned more than £2 a week.[7]

Twenty-seven-year-old Edith, Sarah's youngest daughter, married two days
before D'Arcy on 17 October 1872 at St Paul's, Knightsbridge. Her husband,
the Reverend Charles Gordon Cumming Dunbar, was a younger son of Sir
Archibald Dunbar of Duffus, Morayshire by his second wife. Charles Dunbar
was born on 14 February 1844 at Duffus House, near Elgin. Educated at
Winchester, then by private tutors, in 1863 he went abroad for his health to
India and Ceylon, where in 1867 he was ordained deacon and then priest.
He took up an appointment as domestic chaplain to the Bishop of Columbo
but soon became ill and returned to Scotland. From 1869 to 1871 he was
curate at All Saints', Lambeth and occasionally gave services at Marylebone
Parish Church. In 1871, when Bishop Claughton returned from Columbo,
Dunbar rejoined him as chaplain for his European travels.

Sarah was enthusiastic about a match that was likely to bring Edith a
title, Sir Archibald's eldest son being unmarried. Dunbar, whom Sarah
always called Paul, seemed a good young man who would make Edith happy

and his mother, Lady Dunbar, had none of the grating characteristics of her sister, Georgiana Lowe, whom Sarah had known in New South Wales in the 1840s. It was Georgiana's influence, through her husband Lord Sherbrooke, that Dunbar hoped would procure him a comfortable church living in England. Yet the "silly little High Church curate" seemed an odd choice for the pretty, auburn-haired girl with the rather theatrical mannerisms who had never shared the religious enthusiasm of her sisters.[8]

Exhausted by two weddings, Sarah and Didy were planning to return to Sydney with Laura when Laura suddenly decided that she, too, would marry and remain in England. Laura's fiance was well-known to Sarah. Captain Henry William Keays-Young was the eldest son of Henry Young, formerly chief secretary to the government of Bombay. Born in 1836, he joined the Indian Army in 1856, serving in the Indian campaigns of 1857-59. In 1860 he transferred to the British Army, serving in the 17th Lancers, 18th Foot and the Royal Irish Regiment. Captain Young first met the Wentworths in 1860 and the two families met socially, the Youngs occasionally joining the Wentworths at the opera. Laura's first love had been a devout Roman Catholic. Neither would surrender their religion to marry and Laura had turned her passion to nursing her father. Laura and Harry Young were married at St Paul's Knightsbridge on 17 December 1872, a month after her thirtieth birthday.[9]

So Sarah and Didy returned alone to Sydney aboard the *Bangalore*, arriving on 12 March 1873. Wentworth's remains, together with the marble for the mausoleum, arrived in April aboard the *British King*. Fitzwilliam and Mary were already back in Sydney, where their daughter Dorothy was born in early February. D'Arcy joined them a few weeks later in time for the state funeral of their father. Timmie and her family moved from Vaucluse to the Priory, Fisher's house at North Sydney.[10]

When news of Wentworth's death reached New South Wales, the parliament had decided that he should be given a state funeral, the first ever in the colony. Family disagreements were ignored and Richard Hill, now member of the Legislative Assembly for Canterbury, was appointed one of three commissioners to make the arrangements. Tuesday, 6 May 1873, the day of the funeral, was declared a public holiday. St Andrew's Cathedral was draped with black velvet. So, too, was the polished cedar coffin, decorated with wreaths from the Botanic Gardens and the grounds of Vaucluse.

In the pomp and ceremony of that day, Sarah and her family took a secondary place. In the front aisles sat Robert Hunt, Richard Hill and George Hill, but not Thomas Fisher. The ladies, dressed in deep mourning, sat in the second row — Sarah Wentworth, two Misses Wentworth (Didy and possibly Timmie) and Miss Laura Hill. Fitzwilliam and D'Arcy Wentworth were present as were several other unnamed members of the family. More

State funeral of W.C. Wentworth at St. Andrew's Cathedral,
Sydney on 6 May 1873. *Illustrated Sydney News*, 1873.
State Library of New South Wales.

than 2,000 gentlemen crowded into the cathedral, admitted by tickets issued
by Richard Hill and the other commissioners. Among the throng were the
governor, Sir Hercules Robinson, members of parliament, judges, the university
senate, clergy, foreign consuls and public servants, including Geoffrey Eagar
now Under Secretary for the Treasury, whose half-brother had been fathered
by Wentworth.

After the service, they filed into carriages for a procession to the burial
place at Vaucluse. Spectators, estimated at 60,000 to 70,000, lined the route
along Park and William Streets and into New South Head Road, standing
quietly for more than an hour as the procession passed by. Sydney had
never seen its like. Four hundred colonial born men, wearing rosettes of blue
and crepe and representing community organisations, preceded the hearse,
escorted by mounted police. Then followed the family carriage, coaches of
relatives, the governor and 133 other carriages. An uninvited group of

The Wentworth Mausoleum at Vaucluse. *Vaucluse House Collection.*

mourners, led perhaps by Bobby, joined the funeral procession.

> Much amusement was caused by the appearance of some half-dozen aborigines, following in the procession in the footsteps of the white natives of the colony. They were bare-footed and barelegged, and their dress quaint and motley enough. The spectators were highly amused at the appearance of an item of which no mention had been made in the programme; but it is questionable whether this amusement was shared by the white natives of the colony, whose claims to figure in the procession as "the natives" were thus publicly disputed.[11]

Not since 1831 had such a crowd made its way to Vaucluse. On the hillside east of the house, the vault had been cut out of an enormous rock that looked down over Vaucluse Bay. Here an oration summarising Wentworth's achievements was given by Sir James Martin, and then the coffin, covered with white camelias, was placed in the vault. Steamers at anchor in Vaucluse Bay took the crowds back to Circular Quay and Vaucluse once again was quiet.[12] In a more private moment, the remains of Willie and Belle from England and Joody from Corfu were placed in the vault with their father. Sarah and Didy supervised the work on the mausoleum and the surrounding garden, though little progress was made because, according to

Didy, the workmen were "drunk and away oftener than at work".[13]

Sarah and Didy lived at Vaucluse from March 1873 until early 1875. Fitzwilliam and Mary had leased nearby Greycliffe from Fanny and John Reeve and, though Fitz still made regular trips to New Zealand, Sydney was now their home. With two new grandchildren, D'Arcy, born in 1874, and Fitzwilliam (b.1875), Sarah could enjoy a growing family around her. The older grandchildren — Alice, Robert and Donnelly Fisher — were regular visitors to Vaucluse. Quarrels between the Hills, Hunts, Fishers and Wentworths were laid to rest. Laura Hill was a frequent house guest and companion for Didy while Mary Doyle and her children were again welcome at Vaucluse. Didy, despite her poor health and reliance on medication, was a striking woman with masses of golden hair, large brown eyes and an unpretentious and graceful manner, "a lady in every sense of the term". Now in her mid-thirties, effortlessly drawing the admiration she had once taken such pains to attract, she considered herself past marrying and had accepted the role of companion to her widowed mother.[14]

Sarah was very ill in late 1874.[15] When she recovered her health in the new year, she decided to go to England to see Laura, who was expecting her first child in June 1875, and Edith, whose husband had accepted the position of Archdeacon of Grenada and would leave England later in the year. Family had always been the core of Sarah's world. Widowed, with her children scattered, Sarah became restless to see them. She could afford to travel, and with Joseph Horne appointed resident manager at Vaucluse from 1873, she had no responsibilities to keep her settled in one place. By August 1875, Sarah and Didy were once again living in London hotels, travelling to Ireland, where Laura and her husband were stationed, then back to London to see Fanny and Eliza Wentworth. Laura's health was delicate and her infant daughter survived only a few days. Edith's husband was rector of a church at Hastings from 1873 to 1875, but from 1874 they had leased a house in St George's Square, London. Here Edith and their daughter, Beatrix, born in July 1873, enjoyed a more cosmopolitan life. Sarah joined Edith and her child, known as Dolly, on a holiday in Paris but did not enjoy herself. She disliked Paris and found Dolly a conceited two-year-old who looked too much like her Scottish grandmother.[16]

John Reeve died in London on 21 November 1875. For the last three years of his life he had been paralysed and Fanny had acted on his behalf in all business matters. She and Sir John Darvall, formerly the New South Wales attorney-general, were appointed trustees of his estate. Sarah was concerned that Fanny would not be provided for adequately, "for she is generous and it would pain her to be stemmed."[17] Fanny sold her house in Wimbledon but Sarah's fears were unnecesary. Darvall's advice saved the estate thousands of pounds and later, in 1882, his son married Fanny's daughter Edith Laura. Fanny survived John Reeve by 18 years, proving to be a strong and capable manager not only of her husband's affairs but also of her father's estate. With Fitz mostly in Australia and D'Arcy too irresponsible, it was Fanny who made many day-to-day decisions concerning their investments.[18]

Thomas Fisher also died in 1875, in Sydney on 16 November. Reassured about her daughters in England, Sarah and Didy returned to New South Wales in 1876 to be with Timmie. Sarah always hoped that Timmie would live with her at Vaucluse but her sons preferred that she occupy their father's home at North Sydney. The Priory remained Timmie's home until her death in 1913. Sarah was at Vaucluse throughout 1877 but in February 1878 she was preparing to go to England again. Now aged 73, she explained to her old neighbour, Jane Siddins:

> You will no doubt think it strange that I venture on a voyage so long but my children cannot come to me without great inconvenience and I promised to return if I was spared. I would for my own choice rather remain in My old home for the time I am spared — I feel a stanger in my own country so many of my dear Old friends are gone.[19]

The restlessness had become habit. Didy commented later to Timmie how strange it must be to have a settled home. Sarah Wentworth and Didy sailed for Southampton on the *Avoca* in April 1878. The voyage left them both unwell and seeking medical attention.[20]

Their recovery was not helped by arriving in the midst of a family crisis. Edith and Charles Dunbar had left England in October 1875 but neither liked Grenada and by 1877 they had returned to London. Dunbar went up to Scotland for a year and was offered a church in Glasgow. Edith did not want to live in Glasgow nor did she want to live in India where Dunbar had been nominated for an appointment worth £1,000 per year, so he became assistant at Woburn Chapel in Tavistock Place, London. Prior to his marriage, Dunbar had received an allowance of £200 from his father but this ceased on the day of his wedding. Lacking an income, he borrowed £400 at various stages from Fanny and John Reeve. Edith's considerable income was paid into three accounts — one account for pin money to spend on herself, one account for her husband's use, and a household account into which the bulk of the money was paid.

Dunbar became the preacher at the Tavistock Chapel. He had expected to make £800 a year from this but he got into debt rebuilding the church. When his family would not help him, he drew on his wife's income. Dunbar was a popular preacher, and apart from his tendency to be too lavish with

Vaucluse in the late 1870s. *Wentworth Papers. Mitchell Library.*

Edith's money, Sarah was still fond of him and considered giving him some of her money to help with the church. Edith's money was protected by trust provisions that required that she give her permission for its use. Not wanting to see her husband spend her money on the church, she decided to stop him drawing on her funds and only give him an allowance. In 1878 Edith left Dunbar and took legal action for a judicial separation and custody of her daughter.[21]

February 1880 saw them in court. Fanny, at Edith's request, had taken action against Dunbar to recover money lent to him from Wentworth's estate and she was also claiming a picture belonging to Sarah that Dunbar refused to return. Sarah had been very sick but attended court to give evidence. Dunbar protested that if he had to repay the money he owed Fanny he

111

would be driven to bankruptcy. The jury found in Fanny's favour.[22] Beatrix had been with Edith in August 1878 but went to her grandparents in Scotland. They refused to return the child, holding her to ransom for money to repay their son's debt and accusing Edith of sending five-year-old Beatrix to a school where she had been mistreated. Dunbar gained some public sympathy by claiming that Edith was extravagant and had spent £2,000 on diamonds. This Sarah denied. A glance at the bank books would show it was false. Sarah was horrified by the cruelty of depriving Edith of her child but in her eyes the final wickedness was when Dunbar threatened to make Edith live in two rooms and actually cook for him. Accustomed all her adult life to the luxuries that Wentworth provided, Sarah could not imagine her daughter forced to do manual labour.[23]

Fanny, less emotional than her mother and sisters, blamed Edith. By asking her family to intervene to stop Dunbar's "intolerable tyranny and insults and...his extravagant squandering of her present and future income", she had provoked the archdeacon to fury. Edith had been a forbearing, generous and faithful wife, except for some silly displays of temper which Dunbar had provoked. Fanny's advice to her sister was to withhold all money and she would soon have both a separation on her terms and her child but Edith hesitated, claiming a warm attachment to Dunbar whom she asked to take her back. He refused.[24] Fitz, hurrying half-way round the globe to deal with the crisis, was prepared to compromise and offer Dunbar a small annuity if the child was returned to Edith, "otherwise there will be heaps of dirt necessary to be thrown on both sides". The rest of the family, led by Laura's husband, opposed compromise and they returned to court.

Edith lost her case for custody of Beatrix and for a judicial separation. The child remained with her Dunbar grandparents at Duffus from 1880 until 1893 and neither Edith nor Sarah ever saw her again. Edith eventually settled in Germany where she purchased Burg Schwanegg, an estate near Kissengen, a resort town that she had often visited with her father. Here she died in 1891. In her will she left everything to Didy, apart from generous bequests to her friends Beatrice Dunbar Schulze and Selina Dunbar Schulze.[25]

As well as the tension of Edith's problems, Sarah was worried about Laura's health. The birth of her second child in June 1877 had left Laura in poor health and in late 1878 Didy hurried to Ireland to be with her because she was not well enough to be left alone. Laura's daughter died in February 1879, leaving Laura and Harry broken hearted. Fond of animals, an ardent anti-vivisectionist, Laura "with all her wonderful brain power was such a fragile, tender almost helpless and dependant creature". Her marriage gradually fell apart under the pressure of her ill-health and Harry's drinking. Ignoring her family's advice to leave him, Laura remained with Harry despite

Edith Dunbar (nee Wentworth) (1845-1891) with her daughter Beatrix (b.1873)
and her husband Charles Gordon Cumming Dunbar (1844-1916).
Left: Private Collection; Right: Vaucluse House Collection.

constant arguments and his physical and mental abuse of her. Her death on
her forty-fifth birthday in 1887 was, in the eyes of her brothers and sisters, a
merciful release.[26]

Didy hated the English climate and wanted to return to Vaucluse but,
like Sarah, felt that they could not leave Edith and Laura. News that D'Arcy
would come to England in late 1878 was a further reason for Sarah to stay
but by mid-1879 Sarah considered returning alone. Her health was failing
and she knew if she did not leave soon, she would be too infirm to withstand
the voyage. She hoped that Didy would remain to help Edith, Laura and
her sister-in-law, Eliza Wentworth. Illness prevented Sarah sailing in the latter
half of 1879 and she had to endure another English winter. Though she
claimed to have recovered by February 1880, her health continued to decline.
Didy took her to the seaside at Hastings in March 1880 for a change of air
and with the warmer spring weather she seemed to gain strength.[27]

Sarah realised that she could no longer make the voyage home alone.
She wrote to Timmie, sending money with a request that she come to England
and bring her home to Australia in the southern spring. Fitz supported the
proposal, both as a holiday for Timmie and as support for Didy so they

Without headstone or monument, Sarah Wentworth's grave, Eastbourne, Sussex.
Vaucluse House Collection.

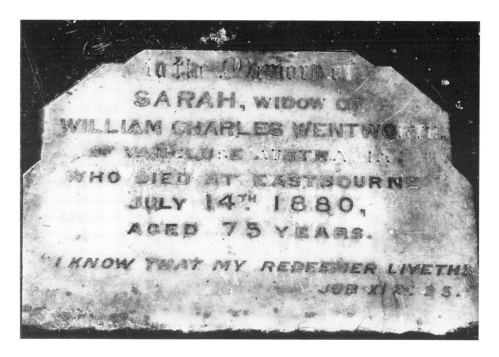

Tablet on Sarah Wentworth's grave. *Photograph in Vaucluse House Collection.*

could get Sarah back to her beloved Vaucluse.[28] In June 1880 Sarah was ill again and her recovery even slower. Now 75 years old, her children feared that she would never regain her strength. Yet her restlessness was still there. Tired of life in suburban London, she sent Edith to look for lodgings at the seaside, at Eastbourne. Fitz watched hopelessly his mother's decline.

> I really do not know what to do or recommend about her — If she could only get a little stronger I should be inclined to advise her to come out direct in the Orient line with myself....it would be a great risk but it must be run if she ever means to see Vaucluse again — otherwise she must wait till October or later and go by the P & O, if she is still alive and strong enough to undertake the journey — It is dreadful to see them all and especially her without a roof they can call their own to cover them — and one is quite helpless to alter this.[29]

Sarah, Didy and Edith rented St Clair House, Eastbourne for the summer but it was already doubtful that Sarah would make her long journey home. She died at Eastbourne on 14 July 1880. Buried in the cemetery of a town she barely knew, far from those she had loved, a small marble plaque marked the passing of Sarah Wentworth, mistress of Vaucluse.

115

REFERENCE NOTES

The major collection of the letters of Sarah Wentworth is held in the Mitchell Library, Sydney at ML A868. The letters were microfilmed (CY POS 725) but were neither arranged chronologically nor paginated prior to microfilming. To assist in locating specific references, the microfilm frame number (fr) has been included as part of the reference.

To avoid confusion and in the interests of brevity,

Wentworth = William Charles Wentworth
Sarah   = Sarah Wentworth (nee Cox)
Timmie   = Thomasine Fisher (nee Wentworth)
Willie   = William Charles Wentworth junior
Fanny   = Fanny Reeve (nee Wentworth)
Fitz   = Fitzwilliam Wentworth
Joody   = Sarah Eleanor Wentworth
Didy   = Eliza Sophia Wentworth
Belle   = Isabella Christiana Wentworth
Laura   = Laura Keays-Young (nee Wentworth)
Edith   = Edith Dunbar (nee Wentworth)
D'Arcy   = D'Arcy Bland Wentworth
Fisher   = Thomas John Fisher
Eliza   = Eliza Wentworth (nee Macpherson, wife of Major D'Arcy Wentworth)

Abbreviations

ML   Mitchell Library
AONSW Archives Office of New South Wales
HRA   Historical Records of Australia
ADB   Australian Dictionary of Biography
RAHS   Royal Australian Historical Society
PRO   Public Record Office, London

CHAPTER 1 — CURRENCY LASS

1 Proceedings of Francis Cox's trial, Crown Minute Book ASSI 2/25, Indictment ASSI 5/110, Public Record Office, Chancery Lane, London; Transportation Registers HO 11/1, p 130 (PRO Reel 87); Bound Indents, AONSW COD 9; A.M. Moore (nee Cox), Diary ML FM3/245; W.A. Pangin, Letter fragment, 191?, Vaucluse House Collection; W.G. Muter, *The Buildings of an Industrial Community — Coalbrookdale and Ironbridge* London: Phillimore, 1979; Ironbridge Gorge Museum, *Teacher's Handbook* n.p.,n.d.

2 Frances Moulton Cranmer appears only in the Transportation Registers HO 11/1, p 206 (PRO Reel 87) and the Ship's Papers (AONSW) but not in the muster for the *Indispensible*; Deed of Settlement between Francis Cox, William Todhunter and George Bloodsworth 1831, ML DOC 405; Sydney Bench of Magistrates AONSW SZ 766 (COD 76) pp 17,21,74-75; AONSW SZ 767 (COD 77), pp 54,101; J. Cobley, *Sydney Cove 1795-1800* Sydney: Angus and Robertson, 1986 pp 232,246,260-61

3 Mutch Index; headstone of Henrietta Hill, Waverley Cemetery

4 Meehan's plan of Sydney 1809; G.P. Walsh, "Manufacturing" in G.J. Abbott & N.B. Nairn, *Economic Growth of Australia 1788-1821* Carlton, Vic: Melbourne University Press, 1969; *Historical Records of Australia*, hereafter *HRA* Series 1, Vol VI p 570; *Sydney Gazette* 13 November 1803, 29 May 1808

5 F. Cox, Memorial, 26 February 1823, AONSW 4/1770, p 114; William M. Cowper, Autobiography, ML A679, pt 11, ch 1; N. Irvine, *Mary Reibey — Molly Incognita* North Sydney: Library of Australian History, 1987 pp 68,77,81

6 *Sydney Gazette* 13 November 1803, 3 September 1809; Sydney Bench of Magistrates AONSW SZ 770 (COD 231); Moore, Diary FM3/245

7 Paylists for 73rd Regiment, PRO Reel 3868; Moore, Diary FM3/245

8 J.T. Bigge, *Report of the Commissioner of Inquiry on the State of Agriculture and Trade in the Colony of New South Wales* Adelaide: Libraries Board of South Australia, 1966 (facsimile edition) pp 70-74; A. Barcan, *A Short History of Education in NSW* Sydney: Martindale Press, 1965 p 28

9 P. Robinson, *The Hatch and Brood of Time* Melbourne: Oxford University Press, 1985 pp 150,154

10 *Sydney Gazette* 19 May 1825; Headstone of Elizabeth Foster, St Stephen's Cemetery, Camperdown

11 F. Cox, Memorials, 26 February, 31 December 1823, AONSW 4/1770 pp 114-15, 4/1836 p 1029; ML DOC 405; *Sydney Gazette* 20 January 1825. There were two men called Francis Cox in New South Wales in the 1820s. One was the Sydney blacksmith, the other a farmer at Wilberforce.

CHAPTER 2 — MISTRESS

1 *Sydney Gazette* 19 May 1825 (This issue was not microfilmed but the original is in Mitchell Library with a photocopy in the Vaucluse House Collection); "T.W.M. Winder", *Australian Dictionary of Biography* hereafter referred to as *ADB* Carlton, Vic: Melbourne University Press, 1967 Vol 2; J.S. Cumpston, *Shipping Arrivals and Departures Sydney 1788-1825* Canberra: Roebuck, 1977

2 "D'Arcy Wentworth", "William Charles Wentworth", *ADB* Vol 2; C.M.H. Clark, *A History of Australia* Carlton, Vic: Melbourne University Press, 1968 Vol 2, p 41 ff

3 C. Liston, 'The Early Career of William Charles Wentworth 1810-1828', B.A.(Hons) Thesis, University of Sydney 1973; *Sydney Gazette* 10 October 1826

4 H. Scott to R. Scott, 8 August 1824, ML A2264

5 W.C. Wentworth, Legal Letter Book, ML A1440 pp 22,34

6 *Sydney Gazette* 15 February 1826; Irvine, *op.cit.*, p 95

7 W.C. Wentworth, Legal Letter Book, ML A1440 pp 41,69,120-21

8 Convict Indent, *Morley*, AONSW 4/4005; Mutch Index

9 W.C. Wentworth, Bank of New South Wales Account Book, ML B1344 (note inside front cover); Mutch Index

10 *Sydney Gazette* 27 September 1826, 17,19 January, 3 March, 25 April 1827; *Australian* 23 November 1827; M. Barnard Eldershaw, *The Life and Times of Captain John Piper* Sydney: Ure Smith and National Trust of Australia (NSW), 1973 p 175

11 W.C. Wentworth, *Australasia*, Barton Papers, Dixson Library MS 68 p 55

12 "Henry Brown Hayes", *ADB* Vol 1; J. Hughes, 'Vaucluse House. Report on Select List of Manuscripts.' Commissioned Report for Historic Houses Trust of NSW, 1982

13 Hughes, *op.cit.*; *Australian* 6, 22, 27 June 1827; Conveyance, Piper to Wentworth, 27 August 1827, Wentworth Family Legal Papers, ML MSS Set 7, Box 1

14 Wentworth to Piper, 30 May 1828, ML A255 p 74; *Australian* 23 November 1827; *Sydney Gazette* 16 May 1828

15 Will of D'Arcy Wentworth, ML MSS Set 7, Box 1; *Australian* 13 July, 7 September 1827; *Sydney Gazette* 14 September 1827

16 A. Macleay to J. Deas Thomson, 8 July 1829 quoted in S.G. Foster, *Colonial Improver: Edward Deas Thomson 1800-1879* Carlton, Vic: Melbourne University Press, 1978 p 21

17 *HRA* 1, X111, p 732; Clark, *op.cit.*, Vol 2, pp 78,82; Mutch Index

18 *HRA* 1, XVI, pp 247-254; *HRA* 1, XV, pp 678-701; B.H. Fletcher, *Ralph Darling: A Governor Maligned* Melbourne: Oxford University Press, 1984 pp 277-79; I.H. Nicholson, *Shipping Arrivals and Departures Sydney 1826-1840* Canberra: Roebuck Society, 1981

19 *Australian* 17 July 1829; *HRA* 1, XV, pp 28-49; "John Stephen", *ADB* Vol 2

20 *Australian* 23 September 1829; Clark, *op.cit.*, p 93

21 Mutch Index; Fanny Catherine Wentworth, Baptism Certificate 1829 (Certified copy 1882), ML MSS Set 7, Box 6. Fanny was christened as Fanny Catherine but usually spelt her name as Fanny Katharine.

22 W.C. Wentworth to D'Arcy Wentworth, 10 April 1817, ML A756; *Australian* 17 June 1847

23 Mutch Index; Clark, *op.cit.*, p 93; N. McLachlan, "Edward Eagar (1787-1866): A Colonial Spokesman in Sydney and London", *Historical Studies*, Vol 10, No 40, May 1963; F. McDonnell, *Portrait of Glebe* Sydney: Ure Smith, 1975 pp 96-97

24 H. Dumaresq to Australian Agricultural Company Directors, 25 February 1836, quoted in D.E. Fifer,

'William Charles Wentworth in Colonial Politics', M.A. Thesis, University of Sydney 1983, p 130

25 F. Macleay to W.S. Macleay, 16 August 1833, ML A4302; *Sydney Herald* 6 June 1833, quoted in Fifer, *op.cit.*, p 224-25

26 G.B. Barton, 'The Life and Times of William Charles Wentworth', Dixson Library MS 69, p 138

CHAPTER 3 — WIFE AND MOTHER

1 Sarah Wentworth to her aunt, 26 June 1831, ML DOC 822; William Nicholas, Sarah Morton Wentworth, water colour portrait c 1852 (private collection)

2 Sarah to her aunt, 26 June 1831, ML DOC 822; *Sydney Morning Herald* 15 January 1848, 19 October 1850; Mutch Index

3 *Sydney Gazette* 21 June 1831; *Australian* 24 June 1831, 19 October 1847; *Sydney Herald* 27 June 1831; ML DOC 121; ML DOC 822; Note with portrait of Mrs R.A. Hunt, Vaucluse House Collection; Unregistered will of Francis Cox with codicil dated 31 October 1828 (private collection)

4 Sarah Wentworth to Thomasine (Timmie) Fisher, n.d. (c 1863), Wentworth Family Letters, ML A868 (fr 675)

5 *Ibid.*

6 Mutch Index; Sarah to Thomas Fisher, 24 November 1867, ML A868 (fr 81 crossed)

7 *HRA* 1, XIX, p 546

8 Robert Brooks & Co. to W.C. Wentworth, 30 July 1841, ML FM4/2348 f 142; AONSW COD 43; Wentworth to W.C. Wentworth junior (Willie), 7 September 1844, ML A756 p 217

9 Wentworth Family Papers, ML MSS Set 8, Box 1, Item 9; Mutch Index

10 AONSW COD 27; Mutch Index

11 Wentworth Family Papers, ML MSS Set 8, Box 4, Item 83

12 Papers of Major D'Arcy Wentworth, ML A755

13 Todhunter was witness to the conveyance from F. McGlynn to W.C. Wentworth, 2 January 1829, Land Titles Office, Book B No 580; *Australian* 9 September 1831

14 "George Hill", "Richard Hill", *ADB* Vol 4; E. Darling to A. Dumaresq, 13 December 1832, ML MSS 2566 p 8; *Sydney Morning Herald* 19 May 1843

15 Fifer, *op.cit.*, p 210

16 *Australian* 19 December 1840; *Sydney Morning Herald* 16 December 1842; "W.T. Cape", *ADB* Vol 1

17 "W.T. Cape", *ADB* Vol 1; Wentworth Family Papers, ML MSS Set 8, Box 1, Item 7; J. Maclehose, *Picture of Sydney and Strangers' Guide in N.S.W. for 1839* Sydney: RAHS and John Ferguson, 1977 (facsimile edition) pp 112-15; Barcan, *op.cit.*, pp 56-57,67,78

18 Receipts and Disbursements for 1844 and 1845, ML MSS Set 8, Box 1, Items 7,8

19 Mrs C. Meredith, *Notes and Sketches of New South Wales* Sydney: Ure Smith and National Trust of Australia (NSW), 1973 pp 45-48; R. Therry, *Reminiscences of Thirty Years' Residence in New South Wales and Victoria* Sydney: RAHS and Sydney University Press, 1974 (facsimile edition) pp 37-38

20 Kinchela to Macleay, 31 October 1831, RAHS MSS B M318; Fletcher, *op.cit.*, p 292; *Australian* 21 October 1831; *Sydney Gazette* 22 October 1831; *HRA* 1, XIV, p 826

21 Governor's Despatches, 19 June 1828 with enclosure, ML A1202 pp 1072-73

22 *Australian* 17, 24 March 1829, 13 January 1830, 3 August 1832; *Vaucluse House* Sydney: Historic Houses Trust of NSW, 1982

23 Wentworth Family Papers, ML MSS Set 8, Box 1, Items 7,8; Assignment Lists, *NSW Government Gazette* 1832; 1841 Census, Household Return No 387, AONSW X950 p 65

24 Sarah to Fisher, 22 May 1868, ML A868 (fr 103)

25 Sarah to Fisher, 23 April, 22, 23 May 1868, ML A868 (fr 98-104)

26 Wentworth Family Papers, ML MSS Set 8, Box 1, Items 7,8

27 *Monitor* 2 December 1835 quoted in Fifer, *op.cit.*, p 245; Therry, *op.cit.*, p 347-51; C.H. Currey, *Sir Francis Forbes* Sydney: Angus & Robertson, 1968 pp 445-48

28 NSW Blue Books 1832-1839

29 *Sydney Herald* 28 September 1835; N.G. Butlin, C.W. Cromwell & K.L. Suthern (eds), *General Return of Convicts in New South Wales 1837* Sydney: Australian Biographical and Genealogical Record and Society of Australian Genealogists, 1987; 1841 Census, AONSW X950 p 65

30 *Australian* 23 October 1835; *Sydney Herald*, 2 November 1835; Colonial Secretary, Letters Received 1835, AONSW 4/2285.2

31 *HRA* 1, XIX, p 630; *Sydney Herald* 7 May 1836; *Australian* 19 July 1836; NSW Legislative Council,

Minutes of Committee on Police and Gaols 1839, pp 88-96

32 *Maitland Mercury* 4 January 1868; C.J. Mitchell, *Hunter's River* Newcastle, NSW: The Administrator of the Estate of Cecily Joan Mitchell, 1984 p 126

33 W.A. Wood, *Dawn in the Valley* Sydney: Wentworth Books, 1972 p 280; J. Atkinson, *An Account of the State of Agriculture and Grazing in New South Wales* Sydney: Sydney University Press, 1975 (facsimile edition) p 77; J. White, *The White Family of Belltrees* Sydney: Seven Press, 1981 pp 24-26

34 Eliza to Timmie, n.d (c.1844), ML A868 (fr 1096-97)

35 Timmie to Eliza, 6 September 1842, ML A868 (fr 1092-95); Wood, *op.cit.*, p 105-6; *Maitland Mercury* 1 December 1848, 4 January 1868

36 Wentworth Family Papers, ML MSS Set 8, Box 1, Items 7,8; Wentworth Family Papers ML MSS Set 7, Box 2; *Sydney Morning Herald* 24 April 1844

37 A. Buck, "Women Property and English Law in Colonial New South Wales", *Law and History in Australia*, Vol 4, 1987

38 Wentworth Family Papers, ML MSS Set 7, Box 4

39 *Sydney Morning Herald* 24 February 1844

40 Wentworth to Willie, 7 September 1844, ML A756 pp 217-19

41 A.P. Martin, *Life and Letters of the Right Honourable Robert Lowe Viscount Sherbrooke* London: Longmans, Green & Company, 1893 pp 287-88

42 Wentworth Family Papers, ML MSS Set 8, Box 1, Items 7,8; Eliza Wentworth to Timmie, n.d. (1844), ML A868 (fr 1087); R. Bedford, *Think of Stephen* Sydney: Angus & Robertson, 1954 p 38; A. Atkinson & M. Aveling (eds), *Australians 1838* Sydney: Fairfax, Syme & Weldon Associates, 1987 p 237

43 Eliza to Timmie, n.d. (1844), ML A868 (fr 1083-85)

CHAPTER 4 — DAMNED WHORE

1 A. Summers, *Damned Whores and God's Police* Harmondsworth, England: Penguin, 1975 p 296

2 E. Darling to A. Dumaresq, 13 December 1832, ML MSS 2566

3 R. Scott to J. Macarthur, 22 July 1833, ML A2955; *HRA* 1, XVlll, p 252

4 *Sydney Herald* 11 February, 3 March 1836; J. Mudie, *The Felonry of New South Wales* Melbourne: Lansdowne Press, 1964 pp 56-57

5 H. Heney, *Dear Fanny* Rushcutters Bay, Sydney: Australian National University Press and Pergamon, 1985 pp 127-28

6 Lady Franklin, 'Journal of a journey from Port Phillip to Sydney 1839', National Library of Australia MS 114. I am grateful to Dr James Broadbent for this reference.

7 A. Atkinson & M. Aveling (eds), *Australians 1838* Sydney: Fairfax, Syme & Weldon Associates, 1987 pp 234-240; L. Davidoff, *The Best Circles. Society, Etiquette and the Season* London: Croom Helm, 1973 p 56

8 Lady Franklin, *op.cit.*; Eliza to Timmie, n.d.(1842-43), ML A868 (fr 1076); E. Windschuttle, 'The New Science of Etiquette' in *Historic Houses Trust Newsletter* No 6 Supplement, December 1985

9 AONSW COD 42; *Australian* 23 October 1841

10 T. Callaghan, Diary 1841-1845, ML A2112/1 p 37

11 Fisher to Timmie, n.d.(1843), ML A868 (fr 1147,1156); Callaghan, Diary, 6 January, 20 June 1843, ML A2112/1 pp 83,131

12 *Sydney Morning Herald* 15 January 1844; Mutch Index

13 W.C. & S. Wentworth to T.J. Fisher, T. Wentworth & D. Wentworth, 12 January 1844, Land Titles Office, Book 6 No 765; Eliza to Timmie, 13 February 1844, ML A868 (fr 1090)

14 Mrs D'Arcy (Eliza) Wentworth to Timmie, 13 February 1844, ML A868 (fr 1089-90)

15 Wentworth to Willie, 7 September 1844, ML A756 p 219; Eliza to Timmie, n.d. (1844) ML A868 (fr 1084,1087)

16 Callaghan, Diary, 23 July 1844, ML A2112/1 p 157

17 *Sydney Morning Herald* 29 October 1844, 14 May 1846; Mutch Index; Fanny to Timmie, 1 August (1868), ML A868 (fr 1062)

18 Norton Smith & Company, Thomas Wardell Papers, ML A5330/2 Items 49,50

19 Wentworth Family Papers, ML MSS Set 7, Boxes 3,4

20 *Sydney Morning Herald* 25 February 1847

21 R.V. Billis & A.S. Kenyon, *Pastoral Pioneers of Port Phillip* Melbourne: Stockland Press, 1974; Bond between Wentworth and Fisher, 22 February 1847, ML MSS Set 7, Box 3; J. Hughes, 'Greycliffe

House — Report on Historical Research.' Commissioned Report for the National Parks and Wildlife Service 1978, pp 2-3,25-28

22 *Sydney Herald* 19 October 1846, quoted in R. Gillespie, *Viceregal Quarters* Sydney: Angus & Robertson, 1975 p 135

23 Gillespie, *op.cit.*, p 139; K.S. Inglis, *The Australian Colonists* Carlton, Vic: Melbourne University Press, 1974 pp 69-72

24 Elizabeth Macarthur to Edward Macarthur, 3 June 1847, ML A2907

25 G.C. Mundy, *Our Antipodes: or Residence and Rambles in the Australasian Colonies* London: Richard Bentley, 1852 Vol 1 pp 371-72

26 *Atlas* 29 August 1846; *Sydney Morning Herald* 9 June 1847; R.B. Walker, *The Newspaper Press in New South Wales* Sydney: Sydney University Press, 1976 pp 37-39; "J. Martin", "A. Michie", *ADB* Vol 5

27 *Atlas* 14 November 1846

28 Blue Books 1846, 1847; "E. Merewether", *ADB* Vol 5; *Atlas* 12 June 1847

29 *HRA* 1, XXV, pp 708-10; Bedford, *op.cit.*, p 58

30 *Sydney Morning Herald* 27 May 1847

31 *Sydney Morning Herald* 27 May, 8,9 June 1847

32 *Australian* 1 June 1847

33 *Australian* 15 June 1847. The other women have not yet been identified. Though not a mother of 20 years, one may have been a sister of Sydney solicitor, Edward Broadhurst. Lowe had made allegations about the immorality of the Broadhurst sisters in 1844. See R. Knight, *Illiberal Liberal* Carlton, Vic: Melbourne University Press, 1966 pp 74-75,122-23

34 *Australian* 15 June 1847

35 *Australian* 17 June 1847

36 Letter from "Epicurus", *Australian* 24 June 1847

37 A.C.V. Melbourne, *William Charles Wentworth* Penrith: Discovery Press, 1972 p 88; Knight, *op.cit.*, pp 179-181; Sarah to Timmie, 3 November 1853, ML A868 (fr 298); Wentworth to Timmie, 31 March 1855, ML A1441, pp 29b-32

38 A. Moore, Diary, ML FM3/245; S. Wentworth, Trust Deed, 9 November 1851, ML MSS Set 7, Box 4; W.C. Wentworth, Will, 11 March 1854, ML MSS Set 7, Box 4

39 *Maitland Mercury* 1 December 1848; White, *op.cit.*, p 35

40 Wentworth to Stirling, 16 November 1850, ML MSS Set 7, Box 4; G. Abbott & G. Little, *The Respectable Sydney Merchant: A.B. Spark of Tempe* Sydney: Sydney University Press, 1976 pp 188-89,191; S.J. Butlin, *Foundations of the Australian Monetary System* Sydney: Sydney University Press, 1968 p 353

41 *Sydney Morning Herald* 2,6 February, 21 April, 15 June, 17 July 1849; Butlin, *op.cit.*, p 354

42 *People's Advocate* 18 August 1849

43 Melbourne, *op.cit.*, p 75

44 *People's Advocate* 25 August 1849

45 James Macarthur to Emily Macarthur, (27?) September 1852 (private collection)

46 A. Barnard, *Visions and Profits: Studies in the business career of T.S. Mort* Parkville, Vic: Melbourne University Press, 1961 p 20

47 C.M.H. Clark, *Select Documents in Australian History 1851-1900* Sydney: Angus & Robertson, 1971 p 697; Wentworth to Timmie, 31 March 1855, ML A1441 pp 29b-32

48 Sarah to Timmie, n.d. (c.1853), ML A868 (fr 481)

49 *Sydney Morning Herald* 19 March 1853; Hughes, 'Vaucluse House', p 107

50 Wentworth to Timmie, 17 March 1854, ML A868 (fr 36); Sarah to Timmie, 3 May 1854, ML A868 (fr 306)

51 Melbourne, *op.cit.*, pp 86-87

52 Wentworth to J. Macarthur, 3 April 1854, ML A2923 p 217

53 *Ibid.*

CHAPTER 5 — COLONIST ABROAD

1 A.M. Moore, Diary, ML FM3/245; Sarah Wentworth to Thomasine (Timmie) Fisher, 3 November 1853, ML A868 (fr 298); W.C. Wentworth to Timmie, 31 March 1855, ML A1441 pp 29b-32; J. Venn (comp), *Alumni Cantabrigienses* Cambridge: Cambridge University Press, 1954

2 Sarah to Timmie, 24 November (1853), ML A868 (fr 699-701); Wentworth to Timmie, 31 March 1855, ML A1441 pp 29b-32; Venn, *op.cit.*

3 Sarah to Timmie, 11 March 1854, ML A868 (fr 304-6)

4 *Ibid.*
5 Sarah to Timmie, 3 May 1854, ML A868 (fr 306)
6 Sarah to Timmie, 3 September 1854, ML A868 (fr 719)
7 Sarah to Timmie, 30 November 1854, ML A868 (fr 722)
8 Wentworth to J. Macarthur, 15 July 1854, ML A2923
9 *Ibid.*; Wentworth to Nicholson, 8 July 1854, ML A756
10 Sarah to Timmie, 30 November (1854), ML A868 (fr 722); Davidoff, *Best Circles*, pp 83-84; M. Wilson (ed. J. Simpson), *A European Journal: two sisters abroad in 1847* London: Bloomsbury Publishing, 1987 pp 19-24
11 Sarah to Timmie, 30 November 1854, ML A868 (fr 722)
12 Wentworth to Timmie, 31 March 1855, ML A1441 pp 29b-32; Sarah to Timmie, 27 June 1855, ML A868 (fr 314-15); E. Macarthur to J. Macarthur, 5 June (1856) ML A2916
13 Sarah to Timmie, 5 November 1855, ML A868 (fr 321)
14 W. Macarthur to E. Macarthur, 17 February 1856 (private collection)
15 A. Oliver to H. Parkes, 8 June 1855, ML A63
16 Sarah to Timmie, 2 December 1855, ML A868 (fr 323-25); A. Moore, Diary, ML FM3/245
17 Sarah to Timmie, 2 December 1855, ML A868 (fr 324 crossed)
18 W. Macarthur to J. Macarthur, 21 September, 16 November 1856, ML A2934
19 Sarah to Timmie, 5 September 1856, ML A868 (fr 326); W. Macarthur to J. Macarthur, 16, 17 November 1856, ML A2934
20 W. Macarthur to J. Macarthur, 16 November 1856, 20 February, 16 March 1857, ML A2934
21 Sarah to Timmie, 23 October 1856, 27 March 1857, ML A868 (fr 279,333); Fitzwilliam (Fitz) to Sarah, 15 October 1856, MSS 217 Vaucluse House Collection; W. Macarthur to J. Macarthur, 16 July 1857, ML A2934
22 Sarah to Timmie, n.d. (August 1857), 20 August 1857, ML A868 (fr 724-25,336)
23 Sarah to Timmie, 20 August 1857, ML A868 (fr 336); Eliza Wentworth to Timmie, 1 January 1856, ML A868 (fr 1077-79); Willie to Timmie, 26 August (1857), ML A868 (fr 996-97)
24 Wentworth to Sarah, 8 December 1857, ML MSS Set 7, Box 4
25 Willie to Timmie, n.d. (Dec 1857), A868 (fr 984-85); Wentworth to Sarah, 3 January 1858, ML MSS Set 7, Box 4
26 *Times* (London) 17, 27 February 1858; Wentworth Family Papers, ML MSS Set 7, Box 4
27 Willie to Timmie, 18 October (1856), n.d. Bayswater (1857-58), n.d. Strand (1857-58), ML A868 (fr 1009-11,1005,990)
28 Sarah to Timmie, 21 July 1858, July 1858, 25 September, 25 December 1858, n.d. (July-December 1858), ML A868 (fr 715-17,346,657-58,348-49,660-61); A. Moore, Diary, ML FM3/245; Will of Sarah Cox, 1888, ML FM3/245
29 Sarah to Timmie, n.d.(1859-60), ML A868 (fr 544)
30 Sarah to Timmie, 25 December 1858, ML A868 (fr 350)
31 Wentworth Family Papers, ML MSS Set 7, Box 4
32 Sarah to Timmie, 23 April, 18 May 1859, ML A868 (fr 353,284-85); Wentworth to Hill, 18 November 1859, ML A68
33 Sarah to Timmie, n.d. (1859-60), n.d. Saturday (1859-60), 26 March 1860, ML A868 (fr 540 crossed, 735-6 crossed,365)
34 Sarah to Timmie, n.d. (August 1860), 3 November (1860), n.d.(December 1860), n.d.(December 1860), 25 December 1860, ML A868 (fr 560,654-55,579,568,378-79)
35 Sarah to Timmie, 25 January 1861, ML A868 (fr 361); R. Therry to J. Macarthur, 24 May 1861, ML A2930

CHAPTER 6 — INTERLUDE: MISTRESS OF VAUCLUSE
1 *Sydney Morning Herald* 19 April 1861; Inglis, *op.cit.*, p 249; W. Macarthur to J. Macarthur 14 (19?) April 1861, ML A2934
2 Sarah Wentworth to Thomasine (Timmie) Fisher, 20 December 1861, ML A868 (fr 376-77)
3 *Sydney Morning Herald* 18 May 1861; Wentworth to Timmie 20 September 1862, ML A868 (fr 50); Sarah to Timmie, 22 September (1861), 20 December 1861, ML A868 (fr 728,374-77); Sarah to Fisher, 26 January 1868, ML A868 (fr 91-92)
4 G.N. Hawker, *The Parliament of New South Wales 1856-1965* Ultimo, Sydney: Government Printer, 1971 p 138; Melbourne, *op.cit.*, p 104; Sarah to Timmie, 21 May 1862, ML A868 (fr 395)

5 Sarah to Timmie, 22 April 1862, ML A868 (fr 390); Sydney Grammar School Archives; E. Windschuttle, "Educating the Daughters of the Ruling Class in Colonial New South Wales 1788-1850", *Melbourne Studies in Education 1980*, p 132; Bedford, *op.cit.*, p 57
6 Sarah to Timmie, 22 September (1861), 21 May 1862, ML A868 (fr 730,394-95)
7 Sarah to Timmie, 22 September (1861), ML A868 (fr 729); Wentworth Family Papers, ML MSS Set 7, Box 4
8 Sarah to Timmie, March 1862, 22 April 1862, 24 November 1867, ML A868 (fr 386,390-91,83); Sarah to Fisher, 26 January 1868, ML A868 (fr 92)
9 Senate Minutes G1/1/-3, University of Sydney Archives; Wentworth to Timmie, 22 September 1862, ML A868 (fr 46); Sarah to Timmie, 22 April 1862, ML A868 (fr 390); R. Therry to J. Macarthur, 11 January 1861, ML A2930; *Empire* 24 June 1862; *Sydney Morning Herald* 24 June 1862
10 Sarah to Timmie, 21 July, 20 September 1862, ML A868 (fr 402 crossed, 406); "T. Barker", *ADB* Vol 1; ML Subdivision Box, Darlinghurst; *Sydney Morning Herald* 20 September 1862; J. Broadbent, "The Push East: Woolloomooloo Hill, the first suburb" in M. Kelly (ed), *Sydney: City of Suburbs* Sydney: New South Wales University Press in association with the Sydney History Group, 1987
11 Sarah to Timmie, 21 July 1862, ML A868 (fr 401); Wentworth to Timmie, 22 September 1862, ML A868 (fr 47); *Sydney Morning Herald* 23 October 1862
12 Young to Newcastle, 21 October 1862, CO 201/523 (PRO Reel 1810); Inglis, *op.cit.*, p 249

CHAPTER 7 — EXPATRIATE
1 *Times* 18 April 1863; R. Therry to J. Macarthur, (17 April?), 19 October, 23 December 1863, ML A2930; G. Macleay to W. Macarthur, 26 May 1864, ML A2954
2 Sarah Wentworth to Thomasine (Timmie) Fisher, n.d. (1864), n.d.(October 1864) ML A868 (fr 633 crossed,534); Sarah to Thomas Fisher, November 1869, ML A868 (fr 155-57); Wentworth to Fisher, 17 May 1870, ML A1441, pp 459-462; Laura Wentworth to Timmie, 23 February (1864), ML A868 (fr 875-76); J. Hutchins, *History and Antiquities of the County of Dorset* Westminster, England: J.B. Nichols & Sons, 1861-73 (3rd edition, 4 vols) pp 304-7; A. Oswald, *County Houses of Dorset* London: Country Life, 1935 p 92; Information from Royal County of Berkshire, County Library, Reading
3 Laura Wentworth to Timmie, 9 February (1864), ML A868 (fr 837-38); Sarah to Fisher, n.d.(1868), ML A868 (fr 269); Wentworth to Fisher, 22 March 1870, ML A868 (fr 26); Sarah to Timmie, n.d. (July 1864), n.d. (1866-67), ML A868 (fr 685,482)
4 Laura to Timmie, 15 July (1864), ML A868 (fr 908,908 crossed)
5 Sarah to Timmie, n.d. (July 1864), 31 December 1867, ML A868 (fr 685,424); Laura to Timmie, 12 April 1865, ML A868 (fr 788)
6 Sarah to Fisher, 28 December 1869, ML A868 (fr 146)
7 Laura to Timmie, Tuesday (December 1864), 23 October (1865), ML A868 (fr 850, 835); Sarah to Fisher, 23 April, 22 May 1868, n.d.(1872), ML A868 (fr 99,101,201); Sarah to Timmie, 2 December 1855, 5 January 1866, 4 November 1868, ML A868 (fr 324 crossed,422,430)
8 Edith Wentworth to Timmie, n.d. (June 1865), ML A868 (fr 1057); Laura to Timmie, 9 February (1865), n.d.(1865), Thursday (1865?), ML A868 (fr 838-39,930-31,953-54); Laura to Miss Perfect, n.d. (1871-72), 3 July (1871-72), ML A868 (fr 944,973); Sarah to Fisher, 24 November 1867, n.d.(late 1869), ML A868 (fr 83 crossed, 264); Sarah to Timmie, n.d.(1867?), ML A868 (fr 575); Wentworth to Timmie, 1 December 1863, ML A868 (fr 51); Wentworth to Fitz, 21 December 1867, ML MSS Set 7, Box 4
9 Sarah to Fisher, n.d. (1870-71), ML A868 (fr 784)
10 Laura to Timmie, 25 September, 7 October 1864, 20 September (1865), ML A868 (fr 775,910-11,821)
11 Laura to Timmie, 12 April 1865, n.d. (May 1865), ML A868 (fr 785,962-63); T.R. Reese, *The History of the Royal Commonwealth Society 1868-1968* London: Oxford University Press, 1968 p 16; D.S. Macmillan, "The Australians in London 1857-1880", *Journal of the Royal Australian Historical Society*, Vol 44, Pt 3, 1958
12 Laura to Timmie, 9 October (1865), ML A868 (fr 805); S. Macarthur to E. Onslow, 21 April 1870, ML A2976
13 Laura to Timmie, n.d. (May 1865), ML A868 (fr 962-63); "The Three Graces", group portrait of Laura, Didy and Edith by H.J. Gruder, painted at the Priory, Alstone, Warwickshire in 1868, Vaucluse House Collection
14 R.A. Hunt, Diary, 3 September 1873, ML MSS 3239/1

15 Laura to Timmie, Monday (1865), 31 January (1865/6), 3 December 1868, 26 January, 29 January 1869, ML A868 (fr 926,860,919,791,857)

16 Laura to Timmie, n.d. (15 March 1865), ML A868 (fr 793)

17 Laura to Timmie, 26 January 1869, ML A868 (fr 791,789 crossed); Wentworth to Timmie, n.d.(1861-62?), Parkes Correspondence, ML A888 pp 314-16

18 Sarah to Timmie, 23 December 1865, ML A868 (fr 414-15); Sarah to Fisher, June 1872, ML A868 (fr 200-1)

19 Sarah to Fisher, 20 April 1869, ML A868 (fr 129-130); Edith to Timmie, n.d.(June 1865), 25 November 1887, ML A868 (fr 1056,1050)

20 Laura to Timmie, 2 July 1864, 10 December (1864), ML A868 (fr 902-3,936); Sarah to Fisher, 28 December 1869, May 1870, 8 September (1870), ML A868 (fr 143-44,147,252)

21 Wentworth Family Papers, ML MSS Set 7, Box 4; Sarah to Timmie, n.d. (late 1864), ML A868 (fr 531); Laura to Timmie, 15 July (1864), 19 December (1864), ML A868 (fr 908,923); Sarah to Fisher, 23 April 1868, ML A868 (fr 98)

22 Sarah to Fisher, 31 December 1867, ML A868 (fr 86)

23 Sarah to Fisher, n.d. (late 1867), ML A868 (fr 590)

24 Sarah to Fisher, 25 August 1867, ML A868 (fr 76-77); Wentworth to Fisher, 22 September 1867, ML A1441 pp 73-80; *Sydney Morning Herald* 24 March 1868; Sarah to Timmie, 30 October 1872, A868 (fr 443)

25 Sarah to Timmie, 21 July 1861, ML A868 (fr 369)

26 Sarah to Timmie, n.d. (October 1864), ML A868 (fr 534); Laura to Timmie, 4 February (1864?), 8 March (1864), 12 March 1865, ML A868 (fr 824-25,879-80,881)

27 Sarah to Timmie, n.d.(1866-67), ML A868 (fr 607); Wentworth to Fisher, 23 August 1867, ML A868 (fr 6); Wentworth to Fisher, 22 May, Power of Attorney 24 July, 23 August 1867, ML MSS Set 7, Box 4; Fisher to Wentworth, 26 February 1866, ML A868 (fr 1152-54); Fisher to Wentworth, 1 August 1868, ML MSS Set 7, Box 4

28 Sarah to Fisher, 24 Sept 1867, ML A868 (fr 89); A.M. Moore, Diary, ML FM3/245; *Jason* arrived in Sydney on 28 December 1866, AONSW Reel 417

29 Wentworth to Fisher, 24 April, 29 June 1867, 24 January, 22 May 1868, ML A1441 pp 49-52,57-60, 97-104,121-24; Wentworth Family Papers, ML MSS Set 7, Box 4

30 Sarah to Fisher, 31 December 1867, ML A868 (fr 84)

31 Sarah to Fisher, 24 November 1867, 25 February 1869, ML A868 (fr 81 crossed,121)

32 Sarah to Fisher, 24 September 1867, 26 December 1868, ML A868 (fr 88-89,94)

33 Sarah to Fisher, 25 June 1867, ML A868 (fr 79); Sarah to Timmie, 26 January 1869, ML A868 (fr 434)

34 During Wentworth's ownership, the property was known as Haddon Riggs. In later years the spelling was changed to Haddon Rig. M. Dormer & J. Starr, *Settlers on the Marthaguy* Dubbo: Macquarie Publications, 1981 pp 13-18,30-31; S. Falkiner, *Haddon Rig. The First Hundred Years* n.p.: Valadon Publishing, 1981 pp 23-29; S.C. Kirby, J.H. McClennan, J. Todhunter, C. Smith, G.S. Brown, Depositions about the death of Willie Fisher 1868, ML A868 (fr 1203-12); *Australian Town and Country Journal* 5 September 1874 p 388 (This issue was not microfilmed but an original copy is held by the State Library of NSW)

35 Laura to Timmie, 16 July, 13 August 1868, ML A868 (fr 846,967)

36 Fanny Reeve to Timmie, 1 August (1868), ML A868 (fr 1061-62 crossed); Laura to Timmie, 13 August 1868, ML A868 (fr 967)

37 Sarah to Fisher, 31 December 1868, 26, 27 January 1869, ML A868 (fr 114,115-16,117-18); Laura to Timmie, 26 January 1869, ML A868 (fr 789); Fitz to Fisher, 5 December 1868, ML A1441 pp 169-72

38 Wentworth to Fisher, 29 July 1868, ML A1441 pp 133-40; Sarah to Fisher, 5 November 1868, 27 January 1869, ML A868 (fr 108,119); Fitz to Fisher, 30 September 1869, ML A1441 pp 355-63; Sarah to Timmie, 28 December 1869, ML A868 (fr 416)

39 Dormer & Starr, *op.cit.*, pp 78-79,102; Falkiner, *op.cit.*, pp 23-29; *Sydney Morning Herald* 6 February 1870; *Australian Town & Country Journal* 5 September 1874; Wentworth to Fisher, 21 April 1870, ML A1441 pp 451-55; Will of Sarah Cox 1888, FM3/245

40 Sarah to Fisher, 31 December 1868, ML A868 (fr 112-13)

41 Sarah to Fisher, 19 May 1869, May 1870, 14 July, 2 November 1870, 20 February 1872, ML A868 (fr 151,147,140-41,134-35,185-86)

42 Wentworth to Fisher, 15 June 1869, ML A1441 pp 295-306

43 Wentworth to Fisher, 10 August 1869, ML A1441 pp 332; Wentworth to Fisher, 17 May 1870, ML

A868 (fr 19-20); Sarah to Fisher, 14 July 1870, 7 September 1871, ML A868 (fr 141,180-81)
44 Fitz to Fisher, 10 August 1871, ML A868 (fr 1110-12)
45 Fitz to Fisher, 1 March 1873 (1872?), ML A868 (fr 1128-29)
46 Sarah to Fisher, 11 May 1872, ML A868 (fr 193-94)

CHAPTER 8 — WIDOW

 1 Fitzwilliam (Fitz) Wentworth to Thomas Fisher, 19 April, 7 August 1872, ML A868 (fr 1113-15,1118);
   Fanny Reeve to Thomasine (Timmie) Fisher, 17 May 1872, ML A868 (fr 672)
 2 Sarah Wentworth to Fisher, n.d. (1872), ML A868 (fr 201)
 3 Fitz to Fisher, 19 April, 5 September 1872, ML A868 (fr 1117-19,1120-24)
 4 Eliza (Didy) Wentworth to Thomasine (Timmie) Fisher, 16 May (1872), ML A868 (fr 1040-44)
 5 Fitz to Fisher, 7 August 1872, ML A868 (fr 1118); Sarah to Fisher, 7 August, n.d. (October-November)
   1872, ML A868 (fr 215,227-28)
 6 Lucy Wentworth to Timmie, 20 September 1873, ML A868 (fr 1101-6); J. Hughes, 'Wentworth Family
   Tree.' Report commissioned by the Historic Houses Trust of New South Wales 1982.
 7 Fitz to Fisher, 5 September 1872, ML A868 (fr 1122); S. Macarthur to E. Onslow, February (1873), A2976
 8 Sarah to Fisher, n.d.(September 1872), ML A868 (fr 219); Sarah to Timmie, 30 October 1872, ML
   A868 (fr 443-44); S. Macarthur to E. Onslow, February (1873), ML A2976; Times (London) 21 January
   1896; Hughes, 'Wentworth Family Tree'
 9 Sarah to Timmie, 30 October 1872, ML A868 (fr 443); Times (London) 30 January 1902; Laura
   Wentworth to Timmie, 12 April 1865, Monday (1865), n.d.(late 1868), ML A868 (fr 786,926,977-78)
10 Hughes, 'Wentworth Family Tree'; AONSW X128, Reel 427; Sydney Morning Herald 29 April 1873
11 Sydney Morning Herald 7 May 1873
12 Sydney Morning Herald 29 April, 7 May 1873; Empire 7 May 1873; Freeman's Journal 10 May 1873;
   Australian Town and Country Journal 10 May 1873; Sarah to Speaker of NSW Legislative Assembly,
   31 October 1872, ML DOC 3265; Wentworth Papers ML A758 pp 183-92
13 Redfern Alexander Accounts, 28 November 1873, ML MSS Set 7, Box 5; S. Macarthur to E. Onslow,
   29 October (1872), ML A2976; R.A. Hunt, Diary, 21 November 1873, ML MSS 3239/1
14 R.A. Hunt, Diary, 21 August, 21 November 1873, ML MSS 3239/1; John Reeve to Fisher, 5 August
   1872, ML A868 (fr 1139-40); Hughes, 'Vaucluse House'
15 R.A. Hunt, Diary, 25 November 1874, ML MSS 3239/2
16 Sarah to Timmie, August 1875, ML A868 (fr 448-50); Hughes, 'Wentworth Family Tree'
17 Sarah to Timmie, n.d. (1876), ML A868 (fr 646)
18 Fanny to Fitz, 16 July 1879 (private collection); Sarah to Timmie, n.d.(1879), ML A868 (fr 489);
   Hughes, 'Wentworth Family Tree'
19 Sarah to Jane Siddins, 6 February 1878, ML MSS 653b; Sarah to Timmie, 5 July (1878), ML A868 (fr
   463-64); Hughes, 'Wentworth Family Tree'
20 Sydney Morning Herald 15 April 1878; Sarah to Timmie, 5 July (1878), ML A868 (fr 462); Didy to
   Timmie, n.d.(1887), ML A868 (fr 1037)
21 Edith Dunbar to Timmie, 5 February (1875-8), ML A868 (fr 861-63); Sarah to Timmie, n.d. (mid
   1878), ML A868 (fr 738-40); Times (London) 21, 23 February 1880, 21, 22 January 1896
22 Times 21, 23 February 1880
23 Sarah to Timmie, 24 March, 24 June, 29 August 1879, 12 March 1880, ML A868 (fr 445-47,469-71,753-57,290-91)
24 Fanny to Fitz, 16 July 1879 (private collection)
25 Fitz to Timmie, n.d.(June 1880), ML A868 (fr 1025); Edith to Timmie, 25 November 1887, ML A868
   (fr 1050); Times 21, 22 January 1896; Will of Edith Dunbar, 20 May 1890, Somerset House, London;
   Beatrix Dunbar to Fitz, 29 March 1895 (private collection)
26 Fitz to Timmie, 11 November 1887, ML A868 (fr 1018-19); Edith to Timmie 25 November, 29
   December 1887, ML A868 (fr 1047-54); Fanny to Timmie, 24 November 1887, ML A868 (fr 1064-70)
27 Didy to Timmie, August (1878), ML A868 (fr 1033); Sarah to Timmie, n.d. (1879?), 13 February,
   12 March 1880, ML A868 (fr 760,289,290)
28 Fitz to Timmie, n.d. (June 1880), ML A868 (fr 1023-24)
29 Fitz to Timmie, 25 June 1880, ML A868 (fr 1021)
30 Will of Sarah Wentworth, Supreme Court of NSW (Probate Division), Series 3, No 5136

BIBLIOGRAPHY

Manuscripts

Wentworth Family Letters and Business Papers ML A868
W.C. Wentworth Legal Letter Book   ML A1440
W.C. Wentworth Business and Estate Papers   ML A1441
Wentworth Family Papers   ML MSS Set 7
Wentworth Family Papers   ML MSS Set 8
A.M. Moore Diary and Cox Family Papers   ML FM3/245
Vaucluse House Collection

Unpublished Theses and Reports

FIFER, D.E. 'William Charles Wentworth in Colonial Politics to 1843', M.A.(Hons) Thesis, University of Sydney 1983

HUGHES, Joy 'Vaucluse House. Report on Select List of Manuscripts.' Commissioned by the Historic Houses Trust of New South Wales 1982

HUGHES, Joy 'Wentworth Family Tree.' Commissioned by the Historic Houses Trust of New South Wales 1982

HUGHES, Joy 'Greycliffe House. Report on Historical Research.' Commissioned by the National Parks and Wildlife Service 1978

LISTON, C.A. 'The Early Career of William Charles Wentworth 1810-1828', B.A. (Hons) Thesis, University of Sydney 1973

Printed Books

DAVIDOFF, Leonore *The Best Circles. Society, Etiquette and the Season* London: Croom Helm, 1973

DAVIDOFF, Leonore and HALL, Catherine *Family Fortunes. Men and Women of the English Middle Class 1780-1850* London: Hutchinson, 1987

GORHAM, Deborah *The Victorian Girl and the Feminine Ideal* London: Croom Helm, 1982

SUMMERS, Anne *Damned Whores and God's Police* Harmondsworth, England: Penguin, 1975

INDEX

Vaucluse 18, 20, 27, 30-33, 42, 59, 70, 77-8, 95, 103, 107, 109; illus 21, 31, 57, 79, 93, 111
Vaucluse Mausoleum 103, 107, 109; illus 102, 108

Wardell, Robert 13, 16, 18, 33, 43
Wentworth, Belle see Wentworth, Isabella
Wentworth, Charles John (John) 16
Wentworth, D'Arcy (son of D'Arcy) 15, 16, 27, 43, 65, 72, 80; illus 14
Wentworth, D'Arcy (son of Fitz) 25, 109
Wentworth, D'Arcy Bland 9, 54, 61, 66, 68, 73, 78, 82, 90, 100, 104, 113; illus 105
Wentworth, D'Arcy Charles (Charles) 16, 26
Wentworth, D'Arcy Dr 15, 16, 18, 70; illus 14
Wentworth, Diana 25
Wentworth, Didy see Wentworth, Eliza Sophia
Wentworth, Dorothy 25, 106
Wentworth, Edith (daughter of Fitz) 24, 100
Wentworth, Edith (see Dunbar) 9, 23, 64, 66, 68, 76, 78, 82, 90, 103, 105-6; illus 89
Wentworth, Eliza Sophia (Didy) 9, 23, 64, 66, 68, 72, 76, 78, 82, 90, 100, 103, 106, 109, 110, 113; illus 74
Wentworth, Eliza (nee Macpherson) 23, 27, 43, 45 ff; 64, 65, 68, 72, 80, 82, 109, 113
Wentworth, Fanny (see Reeve) 9, 21, 23, 28, 46-7
Wentworth, Fitzwilliam (Fitz) 9, 23, 28, 54, 58, 61, 66, 68, 72, 80, 90, 91, 100, 103, 104, 106, 109, 115; illus 92
Wentworth, Fitzwilliam (son of Fitz) 25, 109
Wentworth, George 16, 26, 70
Wentworth, George Godfrey 25
Wentworth, Isabella Christiana (Belle) 9, 23, 64, 66, 108; illus 67
Wentworth, John (son of A. Lawes) 16, 26, 70
Wentworth, John (son of C.Crowley) 16, 27
Wentworth, Joody see Wentworth, Sarah Eleanor
Wentworth, Katherine 16, 26

Wentworth, Laura (see Keays-Young) 9, 23, 25, 64, 66, 68, 76, 78, 82, 86, 88, 100, 103, ·106; illus 75, 99
Wentworth, Lucy Anne (nee Bowman) 25, 104; illus 105
Wentworth, Martha (see Reddall) 16, 26
Wentworth, Mary Ann (see Addison) 16, 26
Wentworth, Mary Jane (nee Hill) 25, 91, 106; illus 92
Wentworth, Nina 25
Wentworth, Robert Charles 16, 26
Wentworth, Sarah Eleanor (Joody) 9, 23, 61, 64, 66, 68, 108; illus 69
Wentworth, Sarah (nee Cox) birth 9; Wentworth's mistress 17; marriage 21; children 23-25; extended family 27-8; dower 37-8; social life 38-9, 41 ff, 85-6; attitude to colony 54, 62, 80; religion 90; business interests 98-100; descriptions 56, 59, 100; portraits 40, 44, 97; health 23, 100, 109, 113; death 115
Wentworth, Sophia (see Towns) 16, 26
Wentworth, Thomasine (see Fisher) 9, 28, 36, 43 ff; illus 37, 44
Wentworth, William C. junior (Willie) 9, 20, 28, 38, 54, 58, 61, 64, 66, 68, 77 ff, 108; illus 37
Wentworth, William C. (son of Fitz) 25, 101
Wentworth, William Charles 9, 13 ff, 62, 66, 76, 77, 80, 83, 85; legal practice 16, 33; legal disputes 70, 72, 83; land ownership 17, 18, 33-6, 55, 56; politics 36, 45, 58-60, 78; health 62, 86-7, 100; death 101; funeral 106-8; character 55-6; portraits 14, 99
Winder, T.M.W. 34
Windermere 33-5, 54, 55
women, attitudes to 22, 41-52, 54, 62, 104
Woolner, Thomas 59

Young, Lady 79, 80; illus 81
Young, Sir John 68, 79, 82; illus 81